IF THIS BE HERESY

IF
THIS
BE
HERESY

JAMES A. PIKE

HARPER AND ROW, PUBLISHERS

NEW YORK, EVANSTON, AND LONDON

All biblical quotations, except when otherwise noted, are from the Revised Standard Version.

LIBRARY OF CONGRESS CATALOG CARD NUMBER: 67-21551

L-R

But this I confess to you, that after the way which they call heresy, so worship I the God of my fathers.

PAUL BEFORE FELIX (Acts 24:14)

ACKNOWLEDGMENTS

In addition to those credited in the dedication with being part of the larger enterprise, I wish to thank others closer to the scene of this immediate task: colleagues at the Center for the Study of Democratic Institutions for their stimulus to creative and critical thought both about ultimate questions and realistic contingent applications, who in different ways in their words and involvement have provided frequent reminders of the "man for others" image; the fellow members of my own family in the Church, the Diocese of California—not the least my successor as *pastor pastorum*—many of whom have similarly nourished my perception of this model and have lovingly ministered to courage in "a time of troubles"—and while under ban in the neighboring diocese in which I reside; my publisher, and especially Messrs. Edward Ziegler and Erik Langkjaer, who have displayed a salutary amalgam of prodding and patience during the research and writing; and the staff of New Focus, my literary and lecture agency, particularly Gertrude Platt and also Joyce Duncan and Carol Householder, who have typed draft after draft and checked and located references, and especially to its director, the late Maren Bergrud, whose degree of collaboration was such that the book can in good measure be regarded as a memorial to her:

requiescat in pace. Thanks are also due to my secretary, Myrtle Goodwin, for ever-ready assistance in this effort and for helping reduce the degree of its subtraction from the fulfillment of my other responsibilities; to Diane Kennedy, on the staff of the First Methodist Church, Palto Alto, sometime exceptional student of mine who contributed sound critique of some of the chapters; to Ann Borg and students on several campuses where I was speaking, for generous sharing in the typing of various drafts; to the faculty, students, and guests at the universities, colleges, divinity schools, and law schools I have been visiting for their stimulating —and often disturbing—questions and statements in response to my presentation of the ideas therein; and to thousands of correspondents and others who this past year, in which its crisis in this country became evident, have been sharing—and informing—my fears for, and hopes for, the Christian Church.

✠ JAMES A. PIKE

Center for the Study of Democratic Institutions
Santa Barbara, California
Ascension Day, 1967*

---

* The ninth anniversary of the author's consecration as a Bishop of the Catholic Church and perhaps the last which, as a clergyman, he may be able to celebrate.

CONTENTS

IF THIS BE HERESY

CHAPTER I

IF THIS BE HERESY

As its period of gestation began, this book was called *Fewer Beliefs, More Belief*. But after a well-publicized event in October, 1966, at which members of the Episcopal House of Bishops taxed me with charges, the relevance of the present title became obvious. Not that this is a book about a segment of the history of the Episcopal Church in which the West Virginia action was (to use a sacramental analogy) both symbol of, and added cause of, crisis in the Church. The almost simultaneous publication of another book by respected and competent chroniclers and analysts[1] relieves me of the necessity of taking space in these pages to cover this complex matter. I am glad to be freed from this burden both because the case in which I am the canonical defendant is still *sub judice* and also because anything more than passing reference to it here and there would obscure the orderly presentation of an approach to belief developed in its main lineaments long before my writing schedule suffered unexpected interruption by a course of events initiated by the circulation of formal heresy charges last September.

[1] William Stringfellow and Anthony Towne, *The Bishop Pike Affair*, Scandals of Conscience and Heresy, Relevance and Solemnity in the Contemporary Church (New York: Harper & Row, 1967). See also Lester Kinsolving, "The Bishop's Not for Burning," *Ramparts*, Jan., 1967.

Yet no ones writes in a vacuum, not least a bishop "out on bail" whose methodology over the years has been shifting from the ontological to the existential, whose focus has been moving (to use words from one of the more acceptable sentences in the House of Bishops' censure resolution) from concern for "traditional propositions about God" to concerns for "faith as the response of the whole man to God." So in an important sense the title of this book has a permeating relevance to the pages which follow. In fact, the whole endeavor can be introduced usefully by analyses inspired by the words of the title.

If. In a free pluralistic society any voluntary association (ecclesiastical or otherwise) is, generally speaking, free to set its own boundaries of membership—and by whatever processes are provided for in its rules and regulations. Such decisions may reflect the wish of the majority of the organization's members, but in more complex structures they need not. It may be that under the bylaws the authority to determine the suitability of one's becoming or remaining a member has been delegated to judicial bodies. While a given decision may seem to relate only to a particular applicant or member, actually the resultant adjudication may express a generic rule which in principle (even if not fully acted out in practice) excludes a whole class of persons, perhaps even the majority. Since all men are fallible, whether acting as members of a majority in the organization's legislative body or as officials of a judiciary, such decisions may be sound or unsound, expedient or inexpedient; nevertheless, in such matters what is, is.

More specifically, in our country, as in most modern nations, each Church is free to be self-defining. Therefore, no individual —whatever his station inside or outside of a Church—has a genuine ground for complaint when on a given occasion a denomination so shapes itself as to exclude him, provided in doing so it has conformed to due process of law.[2] In short, whatever

[2] Church judicial bodies need not follow precisely the procedure established by the state procedural code for criminal prosecutions (to which such

answer the appropriate adjudicatory gives is the right answer. This is the way—and actually the only way—it can be determined whether or not the contents of these chapters are orthodox or heretical, in the common use of these words, as far as the Episcopal Church is concerned.[3] Even the very writing and revising of this book is being done in an interim context—not of my own choosing and somewhat rare in history; the subjunctive introduced by the word "if" will soon be resolved.

---

ecclesiastical disciplinary actions are regarded as analogous), so long as under canon law, and in actual fact, the accused is afforded the fundamental elements of due process, i.e., due notice of the charges and of the preliminary hearings, a trial and appellate hearing, confrontation by his accusers, opportunity for cross-examination and opportunity to have independent testimony introduced in his behalf, plus conformity to any particular procedural guarantees provided by the particular denominational law. The canon law of some bodies, e.g., the Episcopal Church [Canon 53, §7(a)], has provided that the rules of evidence shall conform to those of the state in which the trial is to be held. Although, paradoxically since this important handmaid of justice originated in the medieval canon law, the right of discovery (the right to inspect the prosecution's documents and know of its other evidence in advance) is not provided for in the Episcopal canons, the granting of it would in fact be required in proceedings held in states where this judicial reform has spread through the influence of the inauguration of this procedure as to evidence by the Federal Rules of Civil Procedure [see James A. Pike and John W. Willis, "Discovery under the Federal Rules," (1939) 33 *Columbia Law Review* 1, 89]. In California, for example, a recent Supreme Court decision held that in current proceedings before the Board of Medical Examiners to remove licenses of physicians charged with performing abortions (because of threatened malformation of the child due to the mothers' contracting of German measles), discovery had to be granted the accused even though the right of discovery is not provided for in the regulations of the Board. *Shively and Smith* v. *Stewart, Hearing Officer, and the Board of Medical Examiners*, (1966) 65 Adv. Cal. 514; cf. James A. Pike and Henry G. Fischer, "Discovery against Administrative Agencies," (1943) 56 *Harvard Law Review* 1125.

[3] Accordingly, when the press reported that the Bishop of Arizona renewed the heresy charges in January (oddly enough, *after* the Presiding Bishop had publicly announced the appointment of a distinguished advisory committee to review the broader issues and I had promptly expressed willingness that he defer further the appointment of the first of the judicial bodies), I did not deny his charges: I simply pointed out that the question of whether my teaching is heretical is *sub judice*. As to his vivid attribution of motives, cf. the author's *You and the New Morality— 74 Cases* (New York: Harper & Row, 1967), Chap. 12.

This. This is my fourth attempt to write a book on Christian belief. In the late forties, as a member of the Authors' Committee of the Episcopal Church's Department of Christian Education, I was assigned to co-author the work on doctrine for the Church's Teaching Series.[4] The theological tensions in the Church, at that time focused in the then more polarized Evangelical ("low church") and Anglo-Catholic ("high church") parties, were such that there was a widespread conviction (on occasion shared, it must be admitted, by the authors) that—unlike works on Scriptures, Church history, worship, and the Church "at work"—a book on doctrine could never be written, or that if it could be written it could never survive the steeplechase represented by the committee and sundry groups of consultants of varying categories. But completed and officially published it was—after the effort of about a dozen drafts and ever-improving skill in the art of finding a "form of words," with the length and tediousness of the process rendering the authors more and more numb to the pain of compromise. By this time the much revised text, which had become increasingly uneven in style, was patiently given an attractive editorial polish by one who saved it from disqualification as literature, one who later became our Presiding Bishop, the Right Reverend Arthur C. Lichtenberger. The way the thought of each of the authors has moved in the intervening years (we were paired as the objects of a resolution of censure for heresy—one polite enough to omit our names in patently identifying us—introduced in the House of Deputies at the Detroit General Convention in 1961) has made our capacity or willingness to achieve such a task inconceivable today.

Norman Pittenger was even then, now that I can recognize it, under the wholesome influence of the Roman Catholic Modernist movement,[5] but I was in a phase of development describable as

[4] James A. Pike and W. Norman Pittenger, *The Faith of the Church* (New York: National Council, Protestant Episcopal Church, 1951; 15th printing, Seabury Press, 1966).

[5] In the promising springtime of its post-Conciliar era, now surfacing with creative effect in the Church whose then Pontiff, Pius X, solemnly banned it in 1907.

"smooth orthodoxy."[6] The point is that I was still a lawyer, but one with a relatively new Client. Among my frustrations was the committee's decision that the book for the Church's Teaching Series was not to be a manual of apologetics, but solely a book on doctrine.[7] The chapter headings were phrases from the Nicene Creed; and all was made plausible—with not a little of demythologizing and remythologizing, though at that time I did not know of these words nor was I particularly conscious of the process which they denote. Even this couldn't have gotten us through a few sticky wickets without resort now and again to vague language more homiletical than theological. There are some 139,000 copies of this work about and, though it is the only "Pike and Pittenger" in a literal or historical sense, it is the only over-all doctrinal formulation which our Church with any degree of official sanction has ever issued except for the adoption of the Articles of Religion[8] "established" by the General Convention of 1801.

In the intervening years until 1960 (while I served as Chaplain and head of the Department of Religion at Columbia, as Dean of the Cathedral of St. John the Divine, and began my episcopate in California), involvement in administration, pastoral counseling, and social action made me unaware of the changes in my convictions, changes that had been occurring through continued reading and frequent dialogue with full-time theologians.[9] Then

[6] This approach is also reflected in my *Beyond Anxiety* (New York: Scribner's, 1953), though to a lesser degree since that work was a "private" venture without the values and boundaries of a committee involvement and since it utilized categories of depth psychology and the method of "correlation" learned from a beloved mentor, the late Paul Tillich.

[7] A palliative applied from time to time was a vague assurance that a forensic work could be a later volume in the series. But the Church's Teaching Series was completed and such an additional treatise was never scheduled—for which fact, as its putative author, I am now very grateful.

[8] See pp. 15, 53 f., 64, 65, 67 f., 84 (n.2), and 84 (n. 58), below.

[9] Looking back on it I can now see that the process was well under way in the George Craig Stewart Memorial Lectures I was appointed to deliver at Seabury-Western [Episcopal] Theological Seminary in 1959, published as *A New Look in Preaching* (New York: Scribner's, 1960). The substance of these lectures was again delivered as the Peyton Lectures at the Perkins School of Theology, Southern Methodist University, in 1961.

out of the blue I was confronted with a challenge: an invitation by the *Christian Century* to write a piece in a series entitled "How My Mind Has Changed" (referring to the preceding decade). How much it had changed become evident through the task of fulfilling the assignment.

Between the completion of the article and its publication date in November, 1960, I had the uncomfortable experience of hearing read out at the House of Bishops' meeting in Dallas a proposed Pastoral Letter on doctrine. Surprised by its conservatism (as were many others in the House), I rose to say that if it were passed as it was, I would find myself a heretic. I was referred to a revision session of the drafting committee which attempted to mollify my discomfiture and that of other protesters by a few modifying phrases, such as "St. Luke, for instance, was an evangelist more than a historiographer"—though, since at issue was the draft's flat assertion of the Virgin Birth, which as such was retained, a qualifying reference to St. Matthew (not notably a historiographer) would have been better! Due to what many of us saw as a parliamentary fluke the Pastoral Letter was adopted. (A number were prepared to speak on various points; but after a motion to table was barely defeated, the question on the motion to adopt was immediately put without time for debate on the form of the text.)[10]

After an attack on the *Christian Century* article[11] by the conservative evangelical magazine *Christianity Today*[12] called my views to the attention of a group of South Georgia clergy, I

[10] It was not entirely well received by the Church (it had not been by a good number of the bishops); and some of our priests, contrary to the requirement of Canon 44, §2(f), refused to read it to their congregations, displaying an ecclesiastical form of civil disobedience: e.g., the widely publicized nonfeasance of the Reverend Edward O. Miller of St. George's Church, New York City, one of Manhattan's "cardinal rectors"—as to which the distinguished Bishop of New York, the Right Reverend Horace W. B. Donegan, D. CAN. L., declined to take any canonical action.

[11] November 24, 1960. The article, in somewhat revised form, appears, with the others in the series, in *How My Mind Has Changed*, ed. by Martin Marty (New York: World Pub. Co., 1961), Chap. 10.

[12] January 10, 1961, pp. 20–21.

became the object of widely publicized charges of heresy. But the accusers' bishop eventually decided not to put their petition before the House of Bishops,[13] and as we have already noted in passing, a more vague resolution introduced in the House of Deputies was tabled.

The danger passed, I decided to write a positive book on doctrine (the publishers and I agreed on the title, *I Believe*) which I felt sure would allay any suspicions of heterodoxy. The material was to be organized under phrases from articles of the Apostles' Creed. Not only would there be sound doctrinal affirmation, but this time there would be apologetics—and also, reflecting the rising taste for relevance, a spelling out of the implications for living in each article of the Creed. Hence, each chapter was to have three subheads: WHAT?, WHY?, and SO WHAT? Though the book had almost been completed, only one chapter of the original manuscript survived: an introductory epistemological tract entitled "Why Believe?" It happened that Bishop John Robinson had been kind enough to send me an advance copy of his creative *Honest to God*.[14] As have hundreds of thousands in many countries, I profited from the content, but that is not what primarily affected me. His three main influences, Paul Tillich, Dietrich Bonhoeffer, and Rudolf Bultmann, were already deep in my blood and in my mind. What struck me was the courage of my episcopal brother in *coming right out with it*, a bold statement of a post-Copernican theology—for lay people as well as for professionals.

Earlier a leading American bishop, having heard I was doing another book and assuming that it would be something like the "controversial" article writ large, had sent me a blunt letter urging me not to write it. He said in effect: we know these things, Jim, but don't let "the little people" know. While in my reply I did not accede to this gnostic and condescending distinction (and

[13] The accusers did not ask for the initiation of an "unfrocking" procedure, but rather for some action from the episcopal legislative body. Whether this form of demand was derived from ignorance of canon law or charity I have never known; at the time I thought it was the latter.

[14] London: S.C.M. Press, 1963; Philadelphia: Westminster Press, 1963.

one in the end futile: the little people are getting bigger all the time), I had assured him that in the book-to-be the doctrinal approach would be positive and sound. But now, inspired by *Honest to God*, it became evident to me that before I could get to the positive affirming, all the supposed finalities had to be tested. So for the first time since my days of legal scholarship and writing I employed *Historismus* (the historical method) and a rigorous logic. So what started out as *I Believe* became *A Time for Christian Candor*.[15] Yet as thoroughgoing as was the deabsolutizing, at the end in a chapter entitled "An Apologia for Earthen Vessels" I made a strenuous effort to remythologize the main doctrines. But I couldn't make it with regard to one rather conspicuous doctrine, the Trinity.

At Trinity Church, Wall Street, this topic was the concluding sermon of a series (based on the subject matter of the book) preached during the summer of 1964. The most prompt expression of reaction was the celebrant's unrubrical (but, obviously, for him, urgent) insertion—as a post-Communion collect just before the pontifical blessing I was to give—of the collect for Trinity Sunday:

> Almighty and everlasting God, who has given us thy servants grace, by the confession of a true faith, to acknowledge the glory of the eternal Trinity, and in the power of the Divine Majesty to worship the Unity; We beseech thee that thou wouldst keep us stedfast in this faith, and evermore defend us from all adversities, who livest and reignest, one God, world without end.[16]

But more was to follow. The book didn't come out until near the end of the St. Louis General Convention the next month; but a full account in *The New York Times* of the sermon down at Trinity evoked a public attack from the Anglo-Catholic party organization.

Since I was already scheduled to preach at the Cathedral in St. Louis the day Convention was to open, I took that occasion to seek to support my theological methodology and to articulate

15 New York: Harper & Row, 1964; London: Hodder & Stoughton, 1965.
16 *Book of Common Prayer*, p. 186.

the reasons why many in these days were finding the three-persons-in-one–substance doctrine both noncommunicative and unnecessary. The press elicited from one Missouri bishop warm praise but from another not only condemnation of the preachment, but also denigration of the preacher—including judgmental charges, with a psychoanalytical flavor, about the preacher's motives.

The very next morning the Bishop of South Florida called for the House of Bishops to go into immediate executive session and, after demanding an apology from me in connection with my Cathedral sermon at the nine-thirty corporate Communion of the association concerned with racial justice,[17] he then demanded one for my eleven o'clock sermon on doctrine. The discussion that morning and at a couple of other executive sessions that followed was interesting but indecisive. Yet it affected the context of the next contemplated book. What its title should be also became obvious. As indicated by the chapter title "An Apologia for Earthen Vessels" the guiding text for *A Time for Christian Candor* had been the distinction drawn by Paul (I later learned that its source is in the Dead Sea Scrolls):[18] "For we have this treasure in earthen vessels . . ." So, *What Is This Treasure*[19] became the title of one more well-intentioned effort to set forth a thoroughly positive presentation of the Faith, with a comprehensive coverage of doctrine. Not that I had any thought of recanting; rather, as to conventional doctrines nonaffirmable simply *sub silentio* treatment. But again there was a crucial "moment of truth"—and again, of courage. And again only the first of the originally contemplated chapters survived: the opening one, reporting a genuine pastoral conversation which provided an apologetic for principal doctrines, but that there were so few of these pointed up the reductionism with which I before long found myself charged.

[17] The Episcopal Society for Cultural and Racial Unity, commonly known as ESCRU.
[18] *The Thanksgiving Scroll*, IQH, iv, 5 f., and 27–33.
[19] New York: Harper & Row, 1965.

It happened that for a conference I found it necessary to read, for the first time in many years, Plato's account of Socrates' speeches at his heresy trial and his conversation with a disciple while he was in prison just before his execution.[20] With my mind at that very time on the task of stating a plausible Christology, I could hardly fail to recognize that these speeches were definitely of the same genre as the Passion narratives in the Gospels. Thus the shaft of truth and the strong bolt of courage, both courtesy of Socrates as set down by Plato, emboldened me. So the bulk of the book was devoted to Christology, starting with Square One. Required were new areas of study. And the memory of that rather traumatic literary confrontation kept before me the importance of honesty in the laying of each building block.[21]

Happily, there was time for further revision while I was in England on sabbatical leave at Cambridge. There in the Faculty of Divinity the historical method was primary. Pervasive too was emphasis on semantic and conceptual analysis. So this disciplined approach to affirmations, which had been becoming more operative all through this period of my work, fully surfaced. The latent became manifest. Principally due to the lectures on "The Logic of Theological Statements" by Professor Donald M. MacKinnon (covering some of the ground of the Gifford lectures he was in the midst of giving) and the reading which they inspired, notably Ludwig Wittgenstein's *Tractatus Logico-Philosophicus*,[22] which I read all too late in my intellectual

[20] The Apology and Crito, *The Dialogues of Plato*, translated and edited by B. Jowett (Oxford University Press, 3d ed., 1872), Vol. II.

[21] The penultimate draft of the book was in my briefcase at the 1965 House of Bishops meeting at Glacier Park, to which the Bishop of Arizona brought heresy charges on behalf of a dozen priests. I was given a hearing before the committee (a laudable custom gone extinct by 1966: it did not fit into "the Wheeling dealing") and told them that the manuscript provided a full statement of my present views. "What, another *book!*" was the only interest shown—and that by the chairman, who had not wanted me to write the previous book (see p. 8, above). It was he who in the debate at Wheeling charged me with deceit for silence about the manuscript at Glacier!

[22] Translated by D. F. Pears and B. F. McGuinness (London: Routledge & Kegan Paul, 1961).

history, I became much more sharply conscious of the necessity of distinguishing different types of affirmations and recognizing that the methodology proper to the assessment of one "order" of statement is different from methods appropriate for other types of assertion.

Pondering these categories and methods, I came to the conclusion that of the various types of affirmation—of history, poetry, mythology, ontology, and religious experience—only two were fundamental: ontology, where appropriate (and this in the form of faith-affirmations, to be recognized as such), and history. I had come to the realization that within the latter should be grouped religious experience, since any genuine instance is a datum of history (though not as consensually agreed upon as can be other types of fact); if it happened, it's a happening. Then the other categories of affirmation were for me demoted to a secondary and optional role: myth[23] and poetry are avenues, when appropriate, for the communication of items in the two fundamental categories of history and ontology, fact and faith.

Along with this evaluation came the realization that there was no point in painfully struggling to remythologize what fact and honesty required one to demythologize—that *we should say it the way it is*; then if mythological or poetical imagery now and again provides a helpful way of picturing the truth, all right. But gone for good was the drive—or even the desire—to salvage all the conventional affirmations (as, for example, in the Creeds).[24] The result was a clearer appropriation of the method of reaching theological affirmation which informs the pages that follow—one consonant with the way in which thoughtful men in our times seek to make affirmations in other areas of study and life.

Be. This word emphasizes that fact is at the core of this book. In conventional systematic theology, extended abstractions are

[23] For a critique of my demotion of myth see *Time*, November 11, 1966, pp. 56 ff., at p. 64.
[24] See pp. 58–65, below.

primary. Hence they enjoy a perennial and a fixed status. Yet once it is recognized that affirmations should have a grounding in real data,[25] not in ontological abstractions, it follows that revision of the model may be called for, especially when there is too great a divergence between *what is* and *what is affirmed.*

While, as we shall see, this method does permit one to make affirmations through faith, and then to act upon them, it also obligates one to be open and receptive to new and relevant facts, with all the risks which that entails.

With Albert Camus, then, one embraces the modesty of "we speak what we know." Thus such homilectically impressive phrases as "our unchanging Faith, or "The Faith once delivered to the Saints" become rather hollow.

Yet there is yes-saying in the here-and-now and with the whole heart—and in the real world in which one lives. In so doing, ancient affirmations may well light the way. But no more authority is accorded to them than is warranted by the data which could support an act of faith based on them. The same is true of assertions of even the most persuasive of one's contemporaries or of one's own most attractive analyses.

This approach invites the label "relativism," but it isn't. It is assumed that a body of soundly arrived-at facts will stand behind any belief. More facts constantly press upon us, yet their acceptance does not necessarily erase previously accepted data.

Nor does this method require abandonment of faith-affirmations made on a basis of more limited facts. Fundamental beliefs can well grow more solid when buttressed with new facts. Or, modifications or clarifications may appear appropriate. Further extrapolations may seem plausible; or some reduction in earlier extrapolations may seem desirable. Such a process is meant by the phrase "the development of doctrine" which another Catholic churchman (also having been affiliated with both the Anglican and the Roman Communions), Cardinal Newman, asserted so strongly and persuasively. Even though his view was officially opposed during his lifetime by the Church of his adop-

[25] See pp. 75–81, below.

tion, it is now widely recognized and increasingly utilized. In this process of stability/change, nothing of the true need be lost; more that is true can be known.

Heresy. Under the heading *If* the word "heresy" was used in a commonplace sense and in the light of a realistic recognition of its historic application. We turn to some ancient examples. Increasing research into Christian Judaism shows the prevalence from the beginning of what is now called "angel Christology,"[26] a position of the type expressed later as Arianism and Semi-Arianism, in which Jesus is divine but subordinate to the one God. The action of the First Council of Nicaea automatically made this traditional Christian-Jewish view heretical from the stance of the now larger Gentile Church. But it was not heretical for the ongoing Christian-Jewish groups. When the Nestorian (*two person*) view of Jesus was outlawed through the majority vote of the bishops at the Council of Ephesus in 431, then *ipso facto* it became for the larger segment heretical. But it was—and still is—orthodox in the Assyrian Church. Similarly, when the Monophysite (*one nature*) view of the person of Jesus lost out through the majority vote of the bishops at the Council of Chalcedon in 451, then *eo instanti* for the main body it became heretical. But it was—and still is—orthodox in the ancient Egyptian and Ethiopian Coptic Churches and in the Armenian and Syrian Churches. There was at first permitted, and finally required in the Western Patriarchate, the addition of the *filioque* clause to the Nicene Creed. Since then the affirmation that the Holy Ghost "proceedeth from the Father *and the Son*" became orthodox and has been such for Anglican and Protestant Churches, but it has been heretical—then and now—for the more ancient Eastern Churches.[27]

[26] Cf. Martin Werner, *The Formation of Christian Dogma* (London: A. & C. Black, 1957); Fr. Aloys Grillmeier, s.j., *Christ in Christian Tradition* (London: Mowbrays, 1965); and Fr. Jean Danielou, *The Theology of Jewish Christianity*, Vol. I of *A History of Early Christian Doctrine* (London: Darton, Longman & Todd, 1964).

[27] See also pp. 52, 57, 60, 63, and 66, below.

To take an instance from our era, with the deposition from the priesthood of the Reverend Algernon S. Crapsey, D.D., in 1906,[28] the denial of the literal Virgin Birth and of the physical resurrection of Jesus was made heresy by this canonical action for the Episcopal Church—at least within the New York-New Jersey Province. (The final court of appeal provided by canon law for the discipline of presbyters is provincial;[29] many thought that this particular court was just that—in a sense other than jurisdictional!) On the other hand, after the Church's issuance of *The Faith of the Church*, which allows alternative views on both questions,[30] this judicial definition of heresy might justifiably be seen as in question—even as applicable within the eight New York and New Jersey dioceses.

However, to limit the scope of the word "heresy" to a put-down label for an individual or for a whole national Church caught off base by some official body is to miss the positive meaning most directly derivable from the word's etymology. It comes from a greek noun form (αἵρεσις, *hairesis*) of a verb in the middle voice (αἱρεῖσθαι, *haireisthai*) meaning "to take for oneself"—to choose. This concept corresponds aptly to the conviction that there can be no faith without personal decision. To quote again the words of the important distinction made in the Wheeling censure resolution, without this choosing there can be *assent* to "traditional propositions about God" but not *faith*, i.e., "the response of the whole man." No affirmation, no matter how widespread or official its acceptance, is real or dynamically operative for a person without self-appropriation.

This does *not* mean that each and every official statement (in the Bible, the Creeds, Confessions of Faith, liturgies, etc.) is to be rejected out of hand. Any or all of their sentences, or the purport behind one or many of them, will be accepted as matters of conviction by given individuals. It is a matter of common knowledge, in more recent times confirmed by sta-

---

[28] See also pp. 38 and 64 (n. 29), below.
[29] Canon 53, §4(b).
[30] Pike and Pittenger, *op. cit.*, pp. 86–87 and pp. 100–101, 169–73.

tistics,[31] that Christians, and members of particular denominations—even within the same denomination, vary widely as to how many of the doctrines, represented by official statements, they choose for themselves, *either* in the sense of faith *or* in the sense of assent. It is also a matter of common knowledge that individuals in a given denomination have faith in doctrines or teachings not included in any official statement of their Church. For example, only a minority of Episcopalians believe in the Virgin Birth,[32] which is declared in every one of the types of official statements listed above; at the same time, another minority in the same Church believe in the doctrine of the Assumption of the Blessed Virgin Mary (celebrating it with a Holy Day) and in the Invocation of the Saints (sometimes engaging in the same in public worship)—neither of which doctrines appears in the Bible, the decrees of the Ecumenical Councils, the Creeds, the Prayer Book, or the Articles of Religion, and the second of which is specifically condemned by Article XXII as a "fond thing, vainly invented, and grounded upon no warranty of Scripture, but rather repugnant to the Word of God."[33]

These comments are simply descriptive of the facts. But the positive etymological meaning of the word "heresy" is also of a *normative* character. People should make such affirmations—and only such—as reflect their genuine convictions. As Raynor C. Johnson so aptly puts it:

Men are like children. It is good that they should listen to the voice of external authority and submit to its guidance in the days of their spiritual childhood; but all real development thereafter depends on

[31] See p. 70 (n. 36), below.

[32] Figures as to real degree of belief in this and other conventional doctrines on the part of members of various principal denominations are reported on pp. 69–72, below.

[33] But cf. *The* [Episcopal] *Hymnal 1940*, Hymn 599, stanza 2, which is addressed to St. Mary. The stanza is a "direct paraphrase of the Greek Theotokion, 'Hymn to the Mother of God' sung at the end of each choir office," according to *The Hymnal 1940 Companion* (New York: The Church Pension Fund, 1951), p. 352.

the individual's own untrammeled search, his "endless seeking after endless truth." The fact is that objective formulations of spiritual truth can never be a substitute for experiencing the truth in one's self. These formulations, which are contained in all the scriptures of the world and the commentaries on them, are guides and signposts to the discerning mind. But no belief in historic persons or historic events has in itself power to satisfy the once-awakened hungering soul.[34]

There are, as we shall see, two principal ways people arrive at convictions.[35] If a person's beliefs, however many or few, are to be really his, he should choose maturely which of the two ways appears the more sound and then apply its methodology to select or form such beliefs. This is his *heresy*: his choosing for himself. The results of such choosing may also be heresy in the other, more commonplace, sense of the word. If the denomination to which he belongs officially says that it is, it is. On each such occasion of saying, the given Church is redefining itself. But obviously the Church's action cannot automatically achieve the redefinition of any given person's genuine beliefs. Therefore, if both the positive and negative meanings of *hairesis* are taken into account, *every truly believing individual is heretical* in the positive sense, whether or not what he has chosen to believe is heretical in the negative sense.

[34] *The Imprisoned Splendour* (New York: Harper & Row, 1953), p. 29.
[35] See Chaps. 5 and 6, below.

CHAPTER II

QUALM AND QUEST

Every year the percentage of Christians in the world declines significantly. The greatest cause is the fact that the population is growing at a geometric rate of increase in most countries where Christians of all types taken together represent but a small percentage of the total citizenry. But now even in nations most commonly designated "Christian," Church statistical studies show, in most categories, downward trends—in absolute figures, apart from the population growth factor, which obviously would move the lines on the graph even further away from the horizontal to the vertical direction.

In some countries an increasing *rate* of decline has recently been evidenced. A notable example is England. Its largest Church, the established Church of England, has recently been characterized in a series in the London *Times* as "on the slippery slope." The smaller "nonconformist" Churches are in decline at a not dissimilar rate and feel it more because of the lack of the endowments buttressing the established Church. Cardinal Heenan, the Roman Catholic Primate of England, recently declared that he saw no hope for the future of organized religion in England.

In the United States there was a unique phenomenon after

17

the end of the war, usually referred to as the "religious boom." Statistics in almost every category, and for every principal Church, showed a steady climb. Then these upward curves leveled off in almost every category of church involvement and for almost every Church. Next, Church attendance began to show a steady drop;[1] the same occurred with Sunday School enrollments.[2] During this interim Church membership figures stayed more or less comparable to the rate of population growth (the various categories, for various Churches, running for some years slightly above or for others slightly below, the population increase). But the incongruity between statistics of actual involvement and formal affiliation is explainable by the fact that in virtually all Churches more new members are added to the rolls than inactive ones are dropped.

We are now unmistakably over the crest. The 1967 annual report of the National Council of Churches on the membership of all Churches reveals a decline relative to population growth.[3] And, more than that, the public has rapidly been becoming aware of the Church's waning influence.[4] In 1957 69 per cent of Americans thought that it was "increasing"; but by 1962 only 45 per cent thought so; in 1965 this was the opinion of only 33 per cent, and in 1967, of 23 per cent. As the other side of the coin, in 1957 only 14 per cent suspected that the Church was "losing"; by 1962 31 per cent saw the handwriting on the wall;[5]

---

[1] From 49 per cent in 1958 to 44 per cent in 1965; but, significantly, the drop during this period was 11 points among young adults. Tables prepared by the American Institute of Public Opinion and included in *op. cit.*, n. 3.

[2] E.g., in contrast to population growth, attendance at Methodist Sunday Schools declined during 1966 for the sixth year in a row (almost 3 per cent), and the United Presbyterian Church has suffered a 7 per cent drop over the past two years [UPI dispatch by Louis Cassels, Jan. 14, 1967.] According to the story, "Some believe the postwar religious revival has ebbed to the point where parents who lack a strong personal belief no longer feel under social pressure to take [!] their children to Sunday School."

[3] *The Yearbook of American Churches* (New York: N.C.C.C., 1967).

[4] Gallup Survey released April 11, 1967.

[5] Cf. the author's "Christianity Is in Retreat," *Look*, December 21, 1960,

by 1965, 45 per cent; and in 1967, 57 per cent.[6] But even before these current indications of the over-all trend, two significant harbingers of decline began to be noticed.

First, a rapid decline both in the quantity and in the academic quality of applicants for the ministry became evident. Over-all figures have not yet become available (such as the known 19 per cent drop in the Church of England in 1964, the 38 per cent drop in 1965). But Midwest Roman Catholic dioceses and semi-naries were reported to have dropped 35 per cent in seminarians last fall; and, while the open discussion of the celibacy/marriage dilemma of priests within their Communion accounts for some of this proportion—reports of a not dissimilar decline in other Churches form a frequent part of the conversation of various Church leaders and seminary deans. As to the academic strength of the decreasing number of seminarians there is no reason to assume that peculiar to the Episcopal Church is the ominous situation revealed in May, 1966, by Dr. Nathan M. Pusey, chairman of an Episcopal commission to survey the Church's seminaries: 66 per cent of all seminarians had a C average or less in college—or held no degree at all!

Second, an increasing number of men already ordained are showing disenchantment—a mood often pointedly shown by the growing number entering into specialized work or into secular employment. In a two-year span in the Episcopal Church the total number of clergy not engaged in parish work has increased from 25 per cent to 40 per cent. In the same Church last year fewer men were ordained than in any year since the postwar religious boom got under way.

In all this things seem to be going the same way in Canada.

In earlier periods of history signs such as these would be ones on which those concerned could ponder in a leisurely way. Changes of any kind tended to occur, at most, at an arithmetic

---

reprinted in his *Our Christmas Challenge* (New York: Sterling Pub. Co., 1961), Chap. 1.

[6] Sixty per cent of college graduates were of this opinion, and 63 per cent of young adults (21–29) took this view of the prospects of the Church.

rate of progression. But not so now. Most developments—scientific, technological and social—proceed at a geometric rate. It has been estimated that there has been more actual change in the last twenty-five years than in the whole history of mankind and more change in the last year and a half than in the last ten.

Further, the rapid increase in communications and international mobility means that significant trends in various countries are quickly reflected in other countries. It is not so much a matter of intentional imitation of the resultant patterns as it is the almost inevitable sharing in the ideas, attitudes and practices—sound or unsound—which may bring the same results. Therefore, it is not surprising that marked ecclesiastical declines in country after country—such as France, Sweden, Denmark, Norway, Germany (East and West), England, Australia—have begun to find their counterpart here. So it is far from alarmist to conclude that the Church in this country, too, could in a very short time find itself on "the slippery slope." In any case, in the light of these signs and in the light of the nature of our times, *right now* is time for those concerned for the Church to grasp the significance of the growing diffidence and alienation. Right now is the time for renewal and reformation, and a hard look at the factors in the Church and in the society making for ecclesiastical decline.

The drive so to do need not be stirred only by the negative specter of doom to which the various decline figures point. For concurrent with this downward trend has been an upward one —*a marked increase in interest in religion.* This dual phenomenon has been apparent for some time in England, where the decline of the institutional church was apparent earlier and, as we have seen, has progressed much further. There in the last few years interest in the study of religion at universities—old and new—has resulted in a proliferation of courses; religious broadcasting is widely viewed and heard, and therefore very often it is given prime time; religious books have become more numerous and sell better all the time; informal discussion of religion is becoming more and more widespread.

We are seeing the same trend here. On the increase is the number and size of, and enrollments in courses in, Departments of Religion—within State universities and colleges, as well as within church-related and secular private institutions. (It has been predicted that in four years there will be a shortage of Ph.D.'s in Religion, and well in progress is a "brain-drain" from seminary faculties. There are more and more books and magazine articles in the field of religion.[7]

It is too early to perceive more. But the plain signs of recapitulation in this country of what is already evident elsewhere makes it timely to essay an hypothesis as to the meaning of this apparent paradox.

What these opposing trends seem to be telling us is that *the growing disenchantment with the Church does not mean diffidence toward questions about ultimate meaning.* In fact, the more people are becoming alienated from the institutions which have been the most conspicuous carriers of meanings, or, in other words, the more people conclude—rightly or wrongly—that the Churches have been "tried and found wanting," the greater is the extent of searching via extra-ecclesiastical avenues. And, not surprising should be the fact that where there is the most marked alienation from the Church—among younger people[8]—are found the most discernible signs of religious

[7] Significant, for example, is the frequency of articles on religion and ethics—and by theologians—in what until recently one would have thought a most unlikely forum for such, *Playboy* magazine.

[8] Various recent statistics and estimates show that the sharpest rate of decline is among those under 30. Particularly revealing is the survey of church affiliation among graduate students by Professor Charles Y. Glock and Dr. Rodney Stark (in *Christian Beliefs and Anti-Semitism* [New York: Harper & Row, 1966], pp. 89–90). In the case of students of Roman Catholic, Protestant, and Jewish background, the higher the rating of the graduate school (by American Association of Universities standards) the lower the percentage of active religious involvement. Also, these statistics show that among the students (in the three groups) in the higher-rated graduate schools there is a lower percentage of religious involvement among those who had graduated from higher-ranking colleges (by the same standards) than there is among those who had graduated from colleges of lower standards.

quest. This is one—and an important one—of the several plausible explanations for the rapid increase in the use of marijuana and of psychedelic drugs. While the latter can involve a number of dangers (as an increasing amount of medical data is demonstrating) and while some youthful experimenters, it would appear, are just seeking "kicks," the fact is that for many the motive is the hope for a direct understanding of the meaning of self and one's world, and for personal experience of touching base with whatever is ultimate. (That this hope is not entirely illusory we will see in Chapter 6.)

To use what may seem too crude and vulgar[9] a commercial analogy: That the public may have been put off by, and have lost confidence in, the principal suppliers of a product in a given locality does not necessarily mean there is no market for the product itself. If there is in fact such a market, then, under the circumstances posited, the evidences of interest in it will become all the more apparent. In fact, it is likely that other sources of supply or alternate products which it is hoped will meet the same demand will be strenuously sought.

There are at least three principal operative factors in the growing disenchantment with the institutional Church. We can label these *the performance gap, the credibility gap,* and *the relevance gap.*

Concerning the first, when I summarized recently to one of our Eastern bishops studies which show an *inverse* correlation between the extent of Church involvement and the degree of wholesomeness in socioethical attitudes[10] he replied, "Didn't you know it already, Jim?" It is true that more and more people inside and outside the Church have at some time been sensing what such studies are now confirming. And also more and more in public view is what for some time has been a cause of internal bleeding in the various denominations, individual parishes, dioceses and comparable regional groupings, and national

[9] Two of the qualities of my mode of communication specified by my episcopal brethren at Wheeling.

[10] E.g., see references cited in note 36, p. 70, below.

bodies: conflict between those who want from the Church
mainly *comfort* and those who also want to see it as a *cause*.[11]
It is not surprising then that many who are deeply concerned
about the grave social sins of our day (such as war, racism, and
poverty) use the equivalent of the Biblical text, "By their fruits
ye shall know them" and take a negative view of the Church.

Another way in which the performance gap is growing has
to do with the internal life of the Church itself. At least three
general developments in our culture are operative here: an
increasing moral sensitivity in our society to evils in institutions
generally, an increasing emphasis on the value of human indi-
viduality as compared with the well-being or "safety" of institutions, and increasingly widespread publicity for institutional
failings—both due to the extension of mass media and the
marked increase in the boldness of individuals "to say it the way
it is."[12] Along with this there has been a constant factor inher-
ited from the past: a higher expectancy from the Church than
from "secular" organizations. Taking this all together, not surprising is the growing disenchantment with the Church as it is
more and more found—and exposed—to be in many respects
less moral than other institutions. The rapid increase in specific
critiques of the Church in books and articles,[13] is both a sign

11 *Ibid.*

12 A notable example is the article in *New Blackfriars*, the theological
journal of the English Dominicans, December, 1966, by its then editor, Fr.
Herbert McCabe, O.P., commenting appreciatively on the critique of the
Church by Prof. (formerly Fr.) Charles Davis on leaving the Roman
Catholic Church, with its now famous sentence, "The Church is plainly
corrupt. . . ."

13 For example, "Mother Church is Dead and Gone—What Do the
Children Do Now?" as the working title of *A Church Without God,* by the
Rev. Ernest Harrison, priest of the Anglican Church of Canada (Toronto:
McClelland & Stewart, 1966); *A Modern Priest Looks at His Outdated
Church,* by Fr. James Kavanaugh, priest of the Roman Catholic Diocese of
Lansing (New York: Trident Press, 1967, of which an advance portion
appeared in *Look,* June 13, 1967; Daniel Callahan, "America's Catholic
Bishops," *The Atlantic,* April, 1967, pp. 63–71. Stringfellow and Towne,
op. cit. n. 1, Chap. 1, above; and any issue of the *National Catholic Reporter* and *Commonweal,* national Catholic weeklies, and many issues of
various Church periodicals of the respective denominations.

and a cause of the disenchantment now voiced on every side.

Bearing on the credibility gap[14] has been the rapidly rising level of education, with the result that increasing skepticism and fresh inquiry are replacing conventional acceptance in all realms of thought and conviction. So more and more widespread over recent years have been challenges to specific doctrines—challenges which by and large have been met by representatives of the Church with apologetics or appeals to faith rather than by self-criticism and theological reconstruction.

But what I have noticed—especially in the last year, judging from the nature of questions asked after speeches and in smaller discussion groups—is a marked shift from inquiry about, or attack upon, particular doctrines to more basic questions that challenge the validity of the whole package. Personally I find it paradoxical that, while in my episcopal role in the ecclesiastical "in-group" I am under charges covering such matters as the Virgin Birth, the Trinity, and sole salvation through Jesus Christ, in fact for months now such questions have been very sparse indeed among the hundreds of questions put to me publicly in a wide variety of forums all over the country. Now widening as fast as the credibility gap is *the relevance gap*.

Feeding both the sense of incredibility and the sense of irrelevance are two significant cultural developments in our times: first, what has been called "the authority crisis" and, second, the virtual triumph of the empirical method with its rapid engulfing of more and more areas of human thought and decision-making. These trends show no signs of abating; in fact, they are fast on their way up. Before constructively approaching the bases of belief we should face the reality and implications for the Church and religion of these increasingly significant matrices of contemporary thought and life.

[14] See Fred Kirschenmann, "The Credibility Gap in Theology," *Christian Century*, April 19, 1967, pp. 498–500.

CHAPTER III

THE AUTHORITY CRISIS

Nowadays it's not what you are but what you say and do that counts. One of the rapid shifts of our times is the swift depreciation of status and titles as bases for acceptance of notions.

The change has reflected itself in every phase of society. Take the family. There was a time when most young people accepted something as sound or desirable because parents declared it so to be. Now, by and large, the cause-and-effect relation is reversed. Young people rate their parents' intelligence and good sense in terms of how smart and how sensible they consider their parents' words and actions to be. They may indeed respect their parents; but when they do, it is because their parents' words and deeds are assessed positively on their own merits.

The same is true of other institutions of our society. In the recollection of many of us, there was a time when the fact that the president of a college or university said something made it true for most of the enrolled listeners. Now, more and more such utterances are evaluated on their own merits and the speaker is accordingly assessed; less and less is recognition given to the speaker on the basis of his title with his utterance thus being automatically given credence.

A conspicuous example in American life is what is a more and more widespread mode of response by the public to significant decisions of the United States Supreme Court. As a member of the Bar of this Court I am certainly no less aware than are people generally of the complex apparatus or dignified status symbols with which the Court is provided—the awesome grandeur of the edifice in Washington, the holy of holies mood created by the judicial chamber, the traditional liturgics of the Court's functioning in public. It would take a very fertile imagination to devise more or better trappings appropriate to stimulate a conviction of authority. Now there is no question that in one sense the Court has authority: there are civil or criminal sanctions, which can be backed by force, to effectuate its particular judgments (just like the Church in its heyday.) However, ever since the landmark decision of *Marbury* v. *Madison*[1] the U.S. Supreme Court has had a role much greater in American life than the final settling of certain disputes affecting single individuals and corporations. True, unlike the courts in many states, as provided by special laws, the U.S. Supreme Court cannot issue declaratory judgments but rather can function only in an actual "case or controversy."[2] Yet when such a springboard exists (or is contrived, in order to provide a test case) in a matter involving a constitutional question, the Court's decision can have vast significance, sometimes greater than Congressional legislation— indeed sometimes of the same order of magnitude as Constitutional amendment.

Now, just how authoritative, in terms of public response, is the Supreme Court's functioning in this plenary way? Of course there have always been some critics of its decisions and thus, implicitly or explicitly, of the Justices currently in office,[3] just as there have always been "independent," rebellious children and dissenting college students—even in the era now past when the

---

[1] (1803) Cranch 137, 2 L. Ed. 60.

[2] U.S. Constitution, Art. III, §2.

[3] A long-standing *bon mot* within our profession: the case once decided by the Supreme Court, it still awaits judgment by a higher court—the *Harvard Law Review*.

authority of parents and academic officials enjoyed widespread (almost automatic) acceptance. But in these days—because of the increasing bearing of the Court's decisions on social change, because of a rising level of education and because of more widespread communications—a much higher proportion of the public is involved in the process of response.

As awesome as this body appears, its social policy decisions are not accepted as right, sound, or "constitutional" just because those who have made the decisions are Justices. Vice versa: the public divides, aligning *pro* or *contra* the various judgments on a basis of individually held presuppositions and/or reactions to facts or arguments on the issue (those covered in the Justices' opinion[s] not necessarily being excluded from this category, at least in the case of the more intelligent members of the citizenry), and *thereon* rests the citizens' assessment of the Justices. Thereby the judges are judged—as is clearly indicated in grosser form by expletives ranging from the "Nine Old Men!" cry in New Deal days to the more recent and still current cry of many an ultra-conservative: "Impeach Earl Warren!"

Though fortunately not typical, revealing is a phrase in common use among those of the Radical Right: "the Warren Court." This label precisely exhibits not only what is a special bias in the minds of the speakers, but, more generally, the *way* of evaluation increasingly common on the part of a large proportion of the population: for them the Court has no authoritative status as such; respect or disrespect arises from what the individual men, who happen to be Justices, in fact say and do. For liberals they are just fine when they further the cause of integration, rule out school prayers and Bible reading, and limit police "practices"; they are bad when they permit censorship, as in the Ginsberg (*Eros* magazine) case, or leave undisturbed tax exemption of church properties, as by denying a writ of certiorari in Madalyn Murray O'Hair's suit. For conservatives, vice versa (except for those of the extreme Right for whom the abiding horridness of the Court became an *idee fixe* with the handing down of the first of the school desegregation cases).

Again, as in the other illustrations, the noting of this aspect of the milieu is not for the purpose of endorsing or criticizing any given evaluation of the Court's decisions or of the Court itself. What is relevant for the purposes of our analysis is that there is here a conspicuous example of the over-all trend: selective endorsement or condemnation of various *authorities,* and increasing depreciation of *authority.*

The same has become true in the Church.

The ideas or factual statements of a clergyman, whether parson or primate, were once widely regarded as automatically true. These days having anything from "Rev." to "Most Rev." in front of his name does not produce the former almost Pavlovian response; rather, any reputation he may have for soundness rests upon the fact that a considerable number of things which he has been saying and doing have commended themselves to people in his flock, or beyond.

Nowhere has the development of the authority crisis been more evident than in the Roman Catholic during the last few years. The calling of Vatican Council II by Pope John XXIII can, in perspective, be seen as an effect as well as a cause. It is becoming increasingly evident that in this great Communion of Christians there was already an enormous amount of suppressed restiveness concerning manifold aspects of the Church's doctrinal and ethical teaching, structure and ministry, ways of worship, and practical operations. For many, no longer was it enough that the status quo rested upon the authority of Rome. So on reflection it now would seem apparent that beloved Pope John's then surprising major move toward opening up the whole situation was the only way to begin to ameliorate what would have surfaced before long anyway as an open crisis of authority.

Then, with the door to inquiry now at least ajar, the relatively free discussion of Bishops in Council—made public via the mass media—encouraged Roman Catholic thinkers (from theologians to journalists) to bring various other previously muffled issues even more out into the open. Before long almost everything was under challenge. The inauguration of more democratic policies

—the adoption of the concept of the collegiality of bishops and its implementation through the forthcoming Synod, the organization of national conferences of bishops to exercise a considerable degree of "home rule," the formation of representative bodies on diocesan and parochial levels—represents more than the beginning of a reform in government; channels have now been provided for individuals, clergy and lay, to voice their queries about traditional positions and to propose alternatives. Meanwhile there has been a journalistic transition from "house organs" to a free press and the initiation of new lay-managed papers. The result: more intra-Church controversy is reflected in the pages of Roman Catholic papers and magazines than in all other church publications put together. And Roman Catholic authors have been turning out a spate of books offering candid appraisal and constructive criticism, far ahead in quantity, and often in quality, of critical writing on the part of non-Roman authors (which also, of course, has been on the increase).

The expression of such controversy is not only an effect but also a cause of increasing polarization in the Church between liberals and conservatives, or as they are now frequently called, "post-conciliar" Catholics and "Traditionalists." Obviously aware of the mounting tension, and possessing a more conservative temperament than John XXIII, Pope Paul has in the past year, in statements after statement, increasingly sought to restrain thrusts toward reform and slow up certain movements toward the fulfillment of *aggiornamento* in the doctrinal field.[4]

Not relevant at this point in our discussion is whether the Pope has been wrong or right in any given instance. What is significant, in terms of perceiving the general authority crisis,

---

[4] But he has been impressively bold in some other areas. Repeatedly he has plead for immediate steps for peace in Vietnam (see p. 33, below) and has involved himself and his representatives in the effort. And Pope Paul's recent comprehensive analysis of the world's socioeconomic problems, in the Encyclical *Populorum Progressio*, was sufficiently liberal to be both criticized and praised by many outside and inside the Church as anti-capitalist and Marxist or "marxian."

is the reception accorded these various declarations, and the correlative assessment of the Supreme Pontiff—in Roman Catholic papers and journals of opinion. A few examples will suffice.

His Holiness called a conference of learned scholars in several fields to "update" the Doctrine of Original Sin. In his greeting he reminded them that whatever they discussed or concluded must leave in the picture a single primal couple as the source of original sin. But after he had left, the group promptly proceeded to discuss the subject on the basis of the theory of polygenesis—a posture toward the subject taken for granted by scholars of the caliber of those assembled.

In an address lacking in specificity the Pope warned assembled representatives of the Jesuit Order throughout the world against dangerous trends within the Order. The result? Widespread bewilderment and rebuttal, but no signs of relaxation in the contribution to reform so notably being supplied to the Church by Jesuits.

His Holiness dispatched a strongly worded cautionary message to the Dutch hierarchy on the occasion of their first national conference. But the bishops have since put forth a bold new catechism for adults.[5] It is without an Adam and Eve, a literal Virgin Birth, or a "limbo" for unbaptized children (Heaven is opened for them). They left room for "conscientious" remarriage after divorce, left birth control by the best medical methods to the discretion of the couple, and no longer proclaimed the Atonement a "pay off," but rather an entering by us into the costly commitment of Jesus.[6] In connection with reforms in the teaching and practice in their own country the Dutch hierarchy publicly stated that they wished no interference from the Curia, indicating pointedly that the Church of Holland

[5] *Herder Correspondence*, January, 1967, pp. 3–8.

[6] The approach is based on the challenge in Matt. 20:22b (A.V.): "Are ye able to drink of the cup that I shall drink of, and to be baptized with the baptism that I am baptized with?" and is parallel to the view of the Cross in the Statement of Faith of the United Church of Christ.

did not seek to interfere in the affairs of the Church of any
other country.[7]

Pleas from headquarters for a moratorium on discussion of
the requirement of clerical celibacy have gone unheeded. Roman Catholic scholars and journalists have conducted several
surveys of opinions of priests and of laymen; the results of such
surveys have been given wide publicity within the Church; and
discussion of the pros and cons of the topic have continued to
abound in Roman Catholic publications.

Last year the Sacred Congregation on Doctrine (successor to
the Holy Office, itself successor to the Inquisition) instructed
each national episcopal conference to report on the extent to
which any of a long list of "heresies" were being taught within
the Church in the given country, and what should be done about
it. The French hierarchy's answer deplored the whole idea, declined to heresy-hunt, called for openness to new approaches to
knowledge (to be treated as "sacred") and new foundations for
doctrine and morals, seeing "enthusiastic overstatement" in so
radical an enterprise not suprising—a stimulus and *not* to be
stifled.

As is well known, Pope Paul has for some time had under consideration the matter of a change in the Church's teaching on
birth control. During this period an increasing number of priests,
including some theologians, have taken the position—publicly
and in counseling—that the matter is up to the individual
conscience of married couples since the Church's teaching on
the subject is "doubtful." The bases stated for this claimed
doubtfulness are (a) the fact that the subject has been under
discussion with widely opposing views being presented (this

[7] This is redolent of (but of course not identical with) the quite carefully delimited declaration—considering the temper of the times—of the
bishops and proctors of the Convocations of Canterbury and York in 1534,
which officially marked the beginning of the first phase of the English
Reformation: "That the Roman Pontiff hath not any greater authority
(jurisdiction) bestowed on him by God in the Holy Scriptures in this realm
of England than any other bishop." See Edward C. Rich, *Spiritual Authority
in the Church of England* (New York: Longmans, Green & Co., 1953), p. 18.

would seem to be arguing in a circle!); (b) that an official Papal commission of representative clergymen and laymen was called upon to make a study of the whole question and has made its report, with most of them favoring change; and (c) that the Pope has the matter under consideration and has long been silent on it—some moral theologians arguing that the longer the silence, the firmer the basis for the claim of dubiety: hence freedom of individual conscience. An obvious answer to the argument *sub silentio* would be to say something; and this is exactly what Pope Paul did last fall. He indicated that he was not ready to announce his final verdict but that meanwhile the question was *not* doubtful and that the previous negative teaching was in full force.

Here, as in the other illustrations, the point is not the merit of the matter but how this declaration of the Pope was received. First, the Pope's statement that the question was not doubtful was widely challenged, even in an article in the generally conservative *Our Sunday Visitor*. In effect commentators publicly said, How can he say something is not doubtful on which his own Commission has recommended a change, and which he, himself, is in the very process of weighing? For example, Father Albert Schlitzer, Chairman of the Department of Theology at Notre Dame, declared: "Many Catholics believe that there is still doubt, so it remains a personal choice. A good many theologians would question whether it is a matter of divine law at all. Many Catholics have already made up their minds, and will follow their decisions no matter what the Pope says in the future."[8] Second, continued public comment in church publications and surveys providing indicators of the actual practice and attitudes of Roman Catholics would suggest that the Pope's declaration that the old teaching is still in force has had no marked effect. And the new Dutch catechism, mentioned above, which teaches precisely the opposite, was issued *after* the Pope's statement.

[8] *Time,* April 7, 1967, p. 80.

In 1953 in the Encyclical *Humani Generis,* Pope Pius XII decreed that the philosophy of St. Thomas Aquinas was to be permanently and everywhere accepted as the basis of doctrine; and this particular encyclical did the unusual thing of including an explicit assertion of its own infallibility. Now more and more Roman Catholic theologians not only depart from Thomism in their approaches, but openly disavow it and contradict it on given points or as a system. Yet not a single review or comment the author has seen on the volume most fully denying Thomistic metaphysics, Professor Leslie Dewart's *The Future of Belief,*[9] has challenged it on the authority of Pope Pius XII's encyclical.

However, last winter when Cardinal Spellman called our military forces in Vietnam (Jews, unbelievers and all!) "soldiers of Christ" and urged peace through total victory, liberal commentators did point out the conflict of the Archbishop of New York's statement with the Pope's repeated and urgent calls for a negotiated peace. And, paradoxically enough, conservatives who, by and large, on other matters have been Traditionalist (hence "papalist") praised the Cardinal's position and ignored the Pope's. Here vividly displayed is the change all the examples above are meant to illustrate. *Why* did the liberals prefer the Pope's statement to the Cardinal's? Obviously not on a basis of authority. Rather it was simply because they found what one bishop said more in accord with their view of morals and of reality than they found the other bishop's position to be. And why did the conservatives support the Archbishop's position and despise the Pope's? For precisely the same reason!

Until recently Papal infallibility was viewed by many inside the Church and many more outside to be a block to ecumenism. But it is no longer a problem to the fore. It is abstractly in the picture, but it cannot be conceived of as having any practical relevance now that the papal *magisterium* is so obviously in question—and openly so, within the Roman Catholic Church

---

[9] New York: Herder & Herder, 1966. See also the lecture by the distinguished theologian, Fr. Eulalio R. Baltazer, reported in the *Catholic Star Herald,* March 10, 1967, p. 13.

itself. That the Pope himself is not unaware of this widely discussed authority crisis is evidenced by the noticeable increase
this last year in the number of his authoritarian-sounding cautionary statements,[10] his inauguration of a Year of Faith (with
rationale revealing his deep uneasiness), and his several addresses last Spring on the authority of the magisterium.[11] For example, on April 7, 1967, in an address to the Italian bishops
(though commentators saw it as directed to the Church elsewhere, e.g., Holland and the United States, since he said that
the menacing developments "have not gone far in Italy"), Pope
Paul said: "Something very strange and dolorous is happening,
not only in the profane, unreligious, anti-religious mentality,
but also in the Christian field, not excluding the Catholic camp,
and often—almost by an inexplicable 'spirit of vertigo'—also
among those who know and study the word of God." He referred
to the alteration of the sense of the "unique and genuine faith,"
the most "radical aggressions against sacrosanct truths of our
doctrine," and the questioning of "any dogma that does not
please and that demands a humble homage of the mind to be
received."

"One leaves out of consideration," he continued, "the unsubstitutable and providential authority of the Magisterium; and
one pretends to preserve the title of Christian reaching the extreme negation of any religious content. . . . It is up to us bishops
. . . to take a stand" to combat the "cult of one's own person"
and the spirit of disobedience to the Church that presents the
peril of a "breaking up of doctrine"—which "some feel . . . is
inevitable in the modern world." But in vain, this. When authority is gone, it's gone. Asserting authority authoritatively doesn't
restore it.

It is out of neither bias nor favor that the authority crisis
in one particular Church has been spelled out. It is the largest

10 "These 'go slow' warnings," according to Robert C. Doty, Rome correspondent for *The New York Times* [April 8, 1967, p. 8], "have been in a
ratio of about 3 to 1 to the 'let's get on with council reforms' speeches."
11 *The New York Times, loc cit.;* and the UPI dispatch the same day.

segment of Christendom, and what is happening therein obviously has a bearing on the rest of us. But also it is the Church in which a decade ago one would have least expected such a phenomenon. If sheer authority is not sufficient for unity of conviction in this Church, which had been assessed (too simplistically, it must now be granted) as monolithic, how likely is sheer authority to survive as the basis for certain belief in any other Church?

But lest so much attention in this regard to the Roman Catholic Church give the slightest impression either of prejudice or of myopia as to the operation of the same development elsewhere, now some examples relative to the Episcopal Church.

1. Our more modest version of the Vatican Council, the Lambeth Conference, convened decennially by the Archbishop of Canterbury, in 1920 solemnly declared any and every form of contraception to be sinful. Yet in the years which followed Episcopalians, with practically no pulpit or pastoral condemnation, engaged in birth control in higher percentages than members of most Churches; and from the ranks of the Episcopal Church came a relatively high proportion of leadership in the Planned Parenthood movement. In 1958 Lambeth conformed to the realities, declaring family planning to be a moral obligation.[12]

2. The Apostles' and Nicene Creeds are regularly recited in Prayer Book services, and the House of Bishops has from time to time issued Pastoral Letters (required to be read in all the Churches) as to their authoritative character.[13] Yet fairly recent statistics show that, for example, only a minority of Church members now believe certain of the credal affirmations

[12] In spite of this resolution (and the lack of opposition to its passage on the part of its own archbishop and bishops) the Province of the West Indies condemned contraception at its very next synod.

[13] For example, 1894 ("fixedness of interpretation is of the essence of the Creeds"!), 1923 (regarding the background of, and the reaction to, this rigid declaration issued at a meeting of the House attended by only 65 of the then 140 bishops, see Hugh M. Jansen, Jr., "A Threatened Heresy Trial in the Twenties," *Anglican Theological Review*, January 1967, pp. 17 ff., especially pp. 18–23), and 1960 (see p. 6, above).

used as samples for the study made.[14]

3. The controversy in the Episcopal Church of which the author has been made the focus also provides a telling illustration of the relationship of ecclesiastical authority to the formation of convictions of those who make up the Church. Just as in all the previous illustrations in this chapter, the merits of the matter are not under discussion, nor even the fairness of procedures.[15]

Last September a dozen bishops circulated a draft heresy presentment among the episcopate, picking up only a dozen additional signatures out of a total of 190 bishops. However, since the concept of only three bishops is necessary to initiate the judicial proceedings and since the annual House of Bishops' meeting at Wheeling was but a month away, the Presiding Bishop persuaded the accusers to wait until consideration could be given to the wisdom of a heresy trial in these times. Though three of an ad hoc committee of eight were among the accusers, the author's request for a hearing was unanimously denied; and without any evidentiary process, the committee agreed on a report which, after very limited debate, the House adopted (with minor changes) by a considerable majority. The resolution was a censure of the author—not for heresy, but for conduct: in short, for rocking the boat. This satisfied the accusers; but the author, with the two required episcopal co-signers, initiated judicial proceedings—putting his mitre on the line.

From the vast amount of mail and various sermons and published statements throughout the country it would appear that the judgment of the House was not widely accepted throughout the Church. In fact, last January the Presiding Bishop (not yet having appointed the first of the required judicial bodies), in setting up an advisory committee to study the basic issues (in response the author expressed himself as content that the Presiding Bishop delay further the called-for judicial action), admitted that the censure "had caused confusion and outright disagree-

14 See pp. 69–72, below.
15 As to these aspects of the affair, see the references in n. 1, p. 1, above. As to the procedure, see *You and the New Morality*, pp. 110–18, Case 69.

ment in the Church." This committee, in drawing up its report for the Presiding Bishop, will have had the benefit of a score of position papers from theologians, Anglican and non-Anglican, and personal consultation with four people, including the author. So it is likely that, whatever conclusions are reached, reasoned support for them will be included in the report. It is possible that the conclusions of the committee and of the Presiding Bishop may be such that an endorsement of the report by the House of Bishops at the Seattle General Convention this September would make it possible for the author and his two co-signers to withdraw the canonical demand requiring the judicial process. But for our purposes here let us assume that the latter must proceed. In that case, should the trial stage be reached, full evidence would be adduced in an open hearing publicly reported.

Now involved here, actually and potentially, are three distinct types of processes, enabling us to assess fairly precisely *on what basis* people's convictions are reached within a Church today (not *what* convictions have been or might be reached or their soundness; neither is under consideration in this analysis).

The censure itself, in the first place—the fact of it and of its adoption by the bishops—was not the *cause* of assent or dissent in Church people. Rather, it was vice versa: laymen and clergy liked/disliked the censure, honored/dishonored the censuring bishops (or the minority who opposed the censure), depending on their own feelings toward the censured bishop and his teaching (and upon the degree of their sensitivity about due process).

On the other hand, the committee report may convince some because it includes supporting *reasons* for its action. These reasons—assuming plausibility—are more likely to persuade than the fact that a committee—talented as its members are, and the Presiding Bishop—as distinguished as is his primatial role, will have announced certain conclusions. (It is not likely that with today's mentality they will fare any better, in terms of authority-acceptance, than the Curia and the Papacy are faring these days!)

In the third place, a judicial outcome could be all the more persuasive to the laity and clergy, because in addition to reasoning, judicial opinions, and the like, there would be a full open airing of the *facts*. Yet, since it can be assumed that "the authority crisis" will by that time be still further advanced, it does not seem likely that many will have their doubts settled on the matter simply because a judicial body, official as it is, has announced a yea or nay.

Of the three processes outlined above, the first presented conclusions only. The second will present reasoning and conclusions. The third would involve facts + reasoning + conclusions.

In previous times, conclusions declared by any one of the three instrumentalities of the Church would have been widely accepted as the truth of the matter. Not so any more. The typical person in the Church today is likely to take what facts he knows and, using his own biases and the reasoning of the Church group involved, then form his own judgments of the stature of the members of each deciding body.

The reality of this change of temper was dramatically illustrated in May, 1967, by an impressive service in Rochester (set by Bishop George Barrett of that diocese) in honor of the late Reverend Dr. Algernon S. Crapsey. Sixty years ago Dr. Crapsey was deposed from the priesthood for heresy. The full panoply of canonical judgment, initiated by the present bishop's predecessor, brought about that result.

No one on the more recent occasion (including the author as preacher) said anything judgmental; but the fact of the event itself focused convictions long held by many in the diocese and elsewhere: a convicted heretic was honored; his judges were judged.

Time after time we have seen the Church affected markedly by prevailing cultural patterns surrounding it. From the time a sect of the then-polygamous Jews transmuted into a predominantly Gentile Church conforming to the Greco-Roman norm of monogamy,[16] down to the present day, over and over again we have seen this phenomenon taking place.

16 See the author's *You and the New Morality—74 Cases*, pp. 27–28, Case 25.

To recognize, as a fact, that such changes have taken place, is not to establish that the depreciation of authority is good or right—or bad or wrong. Hence we should move from a descriptive to a normative approach and analyze each of the heretofore respected bases of religious authority, using as ways of assessment both the historical method and logic.

If one or more of these bases holds up, then we should follow it where it leads, and affirm the doctrines thus supported. If none of these systems works, then we should look seriously at another way of arriving at religious affirmations—and if it appears to be sound, we should follow where it leads.

Different churches, and different spokesmen at different times within the same Church, have appealed to one or several of these bases of doctrine: the Bible, the Councils of the Church, the Creeds, denominational Confessions of Faith, particular liturgies, and consensus regarding belief. We now take up each of these categories.

CHAPTER IV

BASES FOR BELIEF

1. *The Bible*

That the Bible *is* the Word of God is the most frequent way of affirming its finality. Somewhat more restrained is the Anglican insistence that it "contains" the Word of God; but as a sometime professor of the author pointed out, this is not intended in the way a haystack contains a needle. Another way of putting it is that the words of the Bible are "inspired" by God. Other traditionalists will grant that the words are really those of the respective authors but insist that all the thoughts expressed are God's thoughts—and hence infallible and final.

> O Word of God incarnate,
> O Wisdom from on high
> O Truth, unchanged, unchanging . . .[1]

"Of making many books there is no end" (Eccles. 12:12b). Why the supremacy of this book? Why not the *Koran* or Ludwig Wittgenstein's *Tractatus Logico-Philosophicus* or Emerson's *Essays*? It does not take a course in logic to see that the acceptance

[1] *The* [Episcopal] *Hymnal 1940*, Hymn 402.

of the Scriptures—either as final or at all—requires some prior (and hence "more" ultimate) ground of authority. Otherwise the claim as to the Bible simply hangs in mid-air.

In answer, those whose faith is Biblicism would assert that the Scriptures are self-authenticating. One support for this position is a text from a relatively late and unknown author: "All scripture is inspired by God."[2]

Two difficulties with this argument are immediately apparent. When the Second Epistle to Timothy was written there was no New Testament Canon; hence it can brace up, at the most, the Old Testament and the Apocrypha. But even about the books contained in these categories a question immediately arises: "What validates 2 Tim. 3:16?" A common answer is that the text, being in the Bible, is inspired—hence conclusive. The circularity of the argument hardly needs exposition.

The only alternative left is that the authors and editors of the Biblical books, and the ecclesiastical officials who put the books in the Canon of Scripture, are infallible.

Here it would be well to recall how the Bible was put together. First of all, very few of the books thereof are of single authorship. Most of them are made up of layers of material. These have been separated with increasing accuracy in the last century or so by a process of literary, linguistic, and historical analysis— not unlike the methodology of geologists and paleontologists— through which underlying oral tradition, separate pieces of writing, penultimate and final editing, and later interpolations can be discerned.

Second, the finished products, the ones which now appear in our Bibles, are simply a number of many sacred writings extant at the various times sorting and selection took place. The first of these latter steps was the work of the rabbinical scholars of the Diaspora in Alexandria, Egypt, who in about the third century B.C.[3] translated a good number of Hebrew writings into

---

[2] 2 Tim. 3:16.
[3] Sometime between the death of Alexander, 323 B.C., and 198 B.C., when Israel passed to the Seleucides.

the Greek patois of the period (called *koinē*),[4] including in their
selection a larger number of writings than ended up in the
official Hebrew Scriptures. The latter were put together by a self-
appointed committee of rabbis of the Pharisaical school who
gathered in a sort of synod after the collapse of the Jewish revolt,
with the destruction of the Temple in A.D. 70 and the fall of
Masada in 73. (It has been usually assumed that this meeting
was at Jamnia, near Joppa, in the late first century.) By vote
they narrowed the number of books; in Judaism the additional
writings found in the Septuagint have been given a somewhat
undefined status and have been designated the Apocrypha.

The earlier (and larger) selection was generally accepted by
the Christian Church. St. Jerome, in his preparation of the
Latin Vulgate directly from the Hebrew version current around
the fourth century A.D., went against the trend: he stuck to the
shorter Palestinian list (adding, however, from the larger Diaspora collection the books of Judith and Tobit). But to his
work were almost universally added the other books—from an
older Latin translation made directly from the Greek Septuagint
—and all the books were accorded equal status.[5] But at the
time of the Reformation the Continental reformers rejected the
Biblical status of the Apocryphal books; and the Church of
England, while retaining them, like Jerome, reduced them to
a secondary status. Meanwhile the Roman Catholic Church has
continued to regard them as being of equal status with the
books of the Hebrew canon.

The anthology known as the New Testament is the result of
the selection of what are relatively few books from a large number of writings in circulation or in possession of local churches
or regional groups of churches. As Principal Adeney and Professor Metzger point out, "The growth and recognition of the
Canon of the New Testament is one of the most important

---

[4] According to Philo, seventy-two scholars in seventy-two days (hence
the approximate designation "Septuagint" or "LXX") working separately
ended up with—by divine inspiration—identical phraseology!

[5] This very fact caused Jews further to minimize them.

developments in the thought and practice of the Church; yet history is absolutely silent as to how, when, and by whom it was brought about."[6] That certain books were regarded as normative and that certain others were not (or in some cases were given secondary standing) is evident from various lists of writings, and from the manner of reference to various books on the part of early Church Fathers and, later on, of a few regional Councils. In the inclusions and exclusions a remarkably wide variety is displayed. To mention just a few examples: Among the inclusions are the Epistle of Barnabas, the Epistles of Clement, the Shepherd of Hermas, the Preaching of Peter, the Didache (the Teaching of the Twelve Apostles), part or all of the Apostolical Constitutions, and the Sibylline Writings. Among the exclusions were Hebrews, Revelation, James, 2 Peter, Philemon, 2 and 3 John, 1 and 2 Timothy, Titus, and Jude.

It appears to be due principally to the thought and work of two figures in the late fourth century, Jerome and Augustine, whose lists happened to coincide, that there developed considerable uniformity. But it was still not complete. For the first six centuries, Syrian Churches omitted four epistles and Revelation. The latter book was not translated into Gregorian until the end of the tenth century; the lateness of its acceptance in the Greek Churches is reflected by the fact that even up to the present it has never been included in their lectionaries. As late as the late fourth century, a Third Epistle to the Corinthians was recognized in Syria and Armenia; and to the present day the Ethiopian Church has retained eight additional books.

As a matter of fact, the only council claiming to be ecumenical to declare on the matter (and it is representative only of the Roman Catholic Church after the Reformation) was the Council of Trent in 1546, which gave to the books of the Apocrypha the same standing as the Old Testament books and lists the New

---

[6] Walter F. Adeney and Bruce M. Metzger, "Canon of the New Testament," in *Dictionary of the Bible*, edited by James Hastings, revised edition, by Frederick C. Grant and H. H. Rowley (New York: Scribner's, 1963), p. 124.

Testament books now customarily accepted.

In the earlier period various selectors (with widely varying selections) articulated various norms for their choices. For example: apostolic authorship, authorship by one who knew an apostle, the degree of consensus among the Churches (with, in the case of Augustine, heavier weighing for the recognition of given books by Churches founded by apostles), etc.

A primary question of authority would be this: By what ultimate norm would one judge which of one or several of these other norms provides an absolute standard? And, apart from this logical problem touching the validity of any or of all such norms, the outcome of their application depends on *facts* as well as on standards. Increasingly scholarship has put in our possession much additional data and the texts (or partial texts) of many additional books written in the same early period—a great many of which contradict or qualify both facts and assumptions which went into the multiform decisions about the Canon of the New Testament.

First of all, it has now long been known that a number of the books selected were in fact not written by those presumed to have been their authors and/or were not composed as early as had been thought. Doubts concerning to the authorship of some books were expressed early. The New Testament scholarship of the last hundred years has not only confirmed these early misgivings but has disestablished the presumed authorship of any number of the books: the apostle John did not write the Fourth Gospel, the epistles known as 1, 2 and 3 John or the Revelation of St. John the Divine; Paul is definitely not the author of Hebrews, 1 and 2 Timothy, or Titus, and is probably not the author of Ephesians and possibly not of Colossians; neither the apostle James nor James, Jesus' brother, wrote the Epistle of James—which is apparently a slightly adapted pre-Christian Jewish tract; the apostle Peter did not write 2 Peter and probably not 1 Peter; nor is the Epistle of Jude attributable to the apostle thus named.

Second, now that a later dating is generally accepted for

most of the books, the hitherto presumed gap between the period covering the writing of the canonical books and the period in which were written other books long known (and grouped for convenience by scholars as the Pseudipigrapha) has been reduced, and in some cases eliminated. And a number of the latter writings also claim to have apostolic authorship.

Third, the discovery in 1945 of the Nag Hammadi writings (strangely enough, the same year as the first discovery of the Qumrân materials, known as the Dead Sea Scrolls) has confronted us with a considerable increase in the number of writings contemporary with the canonical books and the number of those claiming apostolic authorship or origin.[7]

In general these most recently discovered books reflect the point of view known as gnosticism (as do some of the Qumrân passages) in contrast to the predominantly eschatological bent of the canonical books (and of other passages in the Dead Sea Scrolls). A rough and ready distinction between these two outlooks is this: Proponents of the *eschatological* school, while differing widely among themselves as to what precisely is ahead, see the fulfillment of men, or more especially of the Elect, as yet to come through divine intervention into human history—and soon. Proponents of the *gnostic* school regard the consummation as already accomplished; it can be appropriated for present fulfillment by those individuals who *know* the realities (and again here there is a wide range of difference between the features in the scheme and the mode of knowing) and who by faith become part of the consummation.

This distinction is evident throughout from a comparison of the two sets of writings; but a principal example is the matter of the Resurrection. For those of the eschatological point of view the rising again of Jesus established a precedent assuring a final victory to come. Believers who identified with this event

---

[7] James M. Robinson, "Catalogue of the Coptic Gnostic Library" (Claremont, Cal.: mimeo., 1966) and "Kerygma and History in the New Testament" (*ibid.*). See also Thomas C. Oden, "From Event to Language: The Church's Use of Gnostic Mythology," *Religion in Life*, Vol. XXXVI, No. 1 (Spring, 1967), pp. 92–99, and authorities there cited.

were changed because of their confidence in being part of the terrestrially more obvious victory to be achieved by the imminent coming of the Son of Man (by now identified with Jesus) with His angels to reign with His Elect. Meanwhile, the believers—quite aware of lacking, in the remaining days, significant elements of fulfillment—wait in hope. Those of the gnostic point of view, on the other hand, being those fortunate enough to know that they had already participated personally in Jesus' Resurrection (however "spiritually" or literally interpreted), denied that any further *eschaton* was to come, or was needed. They already possessed—or were able to possess—all that could ever be or need to be.

Until recently gnosticism has been seen as a Christian heresy, a later departure from the pristine message borne by the authentic New Testament books and the original teaching of the primitive Church. Since the writings themselves do not display entirely consistent adherence to one of the two philosophies (the larger volume of early writings not selected include some eschatological material; the smaller group of books selected include some emphasis that are gnostic), the books we now call canonical continue to supply texts to support those of gnostic predilection even to the present day. However, since the predominant tenor of the official books is eschatological, it has been possible all along in various ways to wash out the gnostic texts by "interpretation" or now and again by an inconsistent blurring of the two motifs.

Be that as it may, for the purposes of our analysis here the significant thing is that there is no longer a clear basis on which to attribute authenticity to either one of these radically different outlooks as against the other. Until recently it was assumed that by looking at the canonical books one could see, and thus affirm, that the eschatological approach characterized the original message and that the gnostic approach was a later distorting variant attributable to corrupting influences of the milieu into which the Christian movement was more and more entering. Now it is apparent that all along, and before either the writing or the selection of books, each of these contrasting perspectives was widely held by various groups and individuals among the Jews who were focusing their religious responses around the image of Jesus. And now the intensity of the dissension in the primitive Church over this basic matter is evident. And of utmost importance to us today in assessing the normative character of the New Testament is the fact that the process of selection of books was determined by the victory (though not a total one) of one party over the other. To the victor belong the spoils.

It was touch and go: had the gnostic party won we would have by and large a different set of books in the New Testament and the now canonical books thus excluded would be regarded as variant heretical writings. Therefore, the New Testament Canon rather than serving as the ground of decision between two outlooks is the symptomatic result of the victory of one outlook over the other before the selection was made. Anyone making fresh decisions today may opt for one over the other, or discern a "gospel" prior to either, on whatever grounds seem reasonable to him: but no longer open to him as a determinative basis of decision is the mere fact of the inclusion of certain books in what became known as the New Testament.

Contemporary Fundamentalists,[8] whose strongest forte is not

[8] Though they are thought of as very Protestant, it is interesting to recall that neither of the principal Protestant reformers, Calvin and Luther, hesitated to question the authorship of certain New Testament books or to attach varying values to different ones. In this Luther went further than Calvin. As Adeney and Metzger point out, justification by faith (confirmed for Luther by its necessity, nothing else availing, and by its effects) measured the Biblical books: ". . . those Scriptures which manifestly supported the fundamental principle were held to be *ipso facto* inspired, and the measure of their support of it determined the degree of their authority. Thus the doctrine of justification by faith is not accepted because it is found in the Bible; but the Bible is accepted because it contains this doctrine" (Adeney and Metzger, p. 126). Thus outranking all else for Luther were 1 John, Romans, Galatians, and 1 Peter. He called James "a mere epistle of straw compared with them since it has no character of the Gospel in it" (Preface to New Testament, 1522) and said in his preface to this epistle, "I cannot place it among the right canonical works. . . ."

church history, maintain that the Church is founded on the Bible. The plain fact is that the foundation of the people of the Old Covenant (Covenant=Testament) preceded the writing and official selection of the Old Testament; and the Church of the New Covenant[9] was in existence quite a while before the writing in the official adoption of the anthology known as the New Testament. Abraham did not arrive at Beersheba with a copy of the Pentateuch in his luggage; Paul did not distribute pocket Testaments on his missionary journeys. In this regard the Catholic Churches (in the narrower usage—Roman, Eastern Orthodox, and Anglican) have the better case: the Bible is the Church's book. The Bible has no greater authority than the many persons, writers and editors, acting individually as transmitters of oral tradition, and acting individually or corporately as ecclesiastical officials. Unless they are infallible—all of them—the Bible is not infallible.

There is a fascinating anachronism here. Total acceptance of the words of Scripture by particular denominations is, paradoxically, proportional—in an inverse ratio—to distaste for the very *idea* of bishops, councils, and the fixing of liturgical lectionaries (a predominant factor in the process of "canonizing" various books).

Without belief in the infallibility of the Catholic Church or of certain officials within it, how can it be asserted that the Bishop of Hippo and the hermit and papal secretary Jerome and many others of the patristic and early medieval periods who shared in the selection process knew for certain which of the various editors and authors of holy writings were infallible? On what other basis could there be attributed to one or all of these particular writers the gift of inerrancy as compared with other writers in the Hebrew tradition—or for that matter, writers on religious topics in other human cultures? In answer, the dogma

---

[9] Cf. Mark 14:24, A.V.: "This is my blood of the new testament" (i.e., covenant). The New Covenant is one of the names of the Essene sect, whose literature, copies of which have been found at or near Qumrân and at Masada, is popularly called the Dead Sea Scrolls.

that the Jews were the Chosen People, God's unique channel of revelation would be asserted. But where does that doctrine come from? From the Scriptures. Circular reasoning again.

But it is asserted that the Bible is self-authenticating. The Fundamentalists and other conservative "evangelical" Christians assert that the response in the heart of the believer which comes from the reading of the Bible verifies its truth. This is the witness to the Bible. It should be noted that a real truth is being pointed to here. Religious experience in individuals is a *fact;* it is in the category of data. But, as we shall emphasize in a later chapter, there is a generic quality to such instances quite apart from the particular doctrinal system which in any given instance this psychological reality is used to help prove.

Even if one could establish the truth of a given set of words through a positive and fruitful response in an individual who read them and had faith in them, one would have to know in each instance what particular sentences of the Bible were those which achieved these efficacious results. Where indeed would be found verified instances of the life-changing response coming from every single verse between the two covers? How many persons have been reborn from meditating on the last line of Psalm 137 (A.V.): "Blessed shall be he that taketh and dasheth the little ones against the stones"? (This, interestingly enough, in the Anglican liturgy is followed without interruption by the *Gloria Patri.*) How many have been brought to conversion by inspiration from these sentiments of Essene background attributed to Jesus: "For there are eunuchs, that were so born from their mother's womb; and there are eunuchs, that were made eunuchs by men: and there are eunuchs, that made themselves eunuchs for the kingdom of heaven's sake. He that is able to receive it, let him receive it" (Matt. 19:12)? How many have been converted to a style of life of which they would be proud by reading about God's anger at King Saul for not having slain *all* of the enemy when a sense of charity had weakened Saul before his God-assigned task was completed (1 Sam. 15)? How many have been brought to a new level of love of God and

of fellow man by conjoining themselves to the designating of
the Jews as "the synagogue of Satan" (Rev. 2:9b)?

Finally, recognizing no authority or principle[10] superior to
the Bible, the bibliolatrists lack any yardstick with which to
choose between the many contradictory statements in the Scripture. Here the Roman Catholic Church is better off, since it views
the Church as the interpreter of its own books. But then this
solution in turn makes church officialdom the final yardstick, a
position which has problems of its own, as we shall see.

In short, to view the Bible as the infallible norm is necessarily
either to attribute finality to the many persons who put the
Bible together *or* to make an act of faith in the Bible directly
without any underpinnings for the affirmation. If the latter,
there is no more reason to make this act of faith and buy the
whole package than there is to do so in the case of the Koran or
the Book of Mormon—*unless* one can establish that the sentences in the Holy Scriptures are more credible than sentences
in these other "holy" books. But this very process represents an
implicit reliance on some more fundamental norm. Perhaps
even facts? Then the Bible—*qua* Bible—isn't final.

2. *The Ecumenical Councils*

The number of historic Councils of the Church recognized as
ecumenical by the many given segments of the Church depends
upon which of the Councils convened before the given segment
was no longer permitted to attend and be represented. For
example, the Eastern Orthodox Churches recognize as ecumenical all the Councils before the split between the Eastern
and Western Christendom in the eleventh century, and do not
recognize as ecumenical the Councils of the Western bishops from
that time on. The Assyrian Church, which was separated from
the rest of the Church after the condemnation of its Nestorian
doctrine (that is, that Jesus Christ is two persons—one divine,
and one human), recognizes none of the Councils after the

10 In contrast to Luther: see n. 8, above.

Council of Ephesus in 431 condemned this particular "heresy."
Similarly the Coptic Churches of Egypt and Ethiopia and the
Armenian Church, which continued their adherence to Monophysite doctrine (just the opposite of Nestorianism: Jesus as
one person with one nature—both human and divine), recognize no Councils after the condemnation of this view. So, too
the Church of England has not recognized as ecumenical the
Councils of the Church of Rome occurring after the separation
of the two Churches: the Council of Trent, Vatican Council I,
and Vatican Council II.

The Church of England and the new Churches of the Reforma-
tion went further, however. Logically it would be thought that
they would recognize as valid councils such as the Fourth
Lateran Council (1215), the Council of Pisa (1414), and the
Council of Florence (1445), all of which occurred after the
East–West schism but before the time of the Reformation.
They have not done so. Though there was little or no contact be-
tween the European Churches which broke with Rome at the
Reformation and the Eastern Orthodox Church, these Western
Churches in fact adopted the same norm as the Eastern Orthodox
Church in limiting their recognition of Councils to those occurring before the East–West schism. The Anglican Church, the
Lutheran Churches, and the Reformed Churches felt free to
reject the doctrine of transubstantiation although it was affirmed
by the Fourth Lateran Council at a time when the forebears
in each of these groups were represented. At the same time
these Churches did not challenge those decrees of the Councils,
held before the Great Schism, which had developed the Doctrine
of the Trinity and the classical Christology. On the contrary:
these formulations were accepted fully, in fact reaffirmed, in
the Confessions of Faith of the Reformation period. And appeal
to the authority of the Councils has been quite common at times
of later theological controversy within these Churches. Because
of this, it is widely assumed that Councils represent a yardstick,
alongside the yardstick of the Bible, for those Churches which
became autonomous at the time of the Reformation. Whether

or not this is really the official position of these Churches we shall see. But assuming that to be the case for the moment, the fact that the earlier Councils seem to be accepted and that other Councils of a date later but still before these Churches became separate seem not accepted makes it obvious that there is some more fundamental norm by which Councils themselves are judged.

The absence of the Eastern Orthodox bishops from the Fourth Lateran Council would at the time of the Reformation have had no great significance to the reformers, since they were out of touch with the Eastern Church anyway and had no particular interest in the precise theological issue which had divided East and West. The issue was the addition by the Western Church of the *filioque* to the Creed. The conciliar form of the article in question was "I believe in the Holy Ghost . . . who proceedeth from the Father." The words "and the Son" were added only in the West, without a decision of an Ecumenical Council. The acceptance of these additional words resulted in the mutual excommunications visited upon each other by the Bishop of Rome and the Patriarch of Constantinople. Yet this expanded form of the Nicene Creed continued past the Reformation to the present day,[11] the question not even having been raised at the time of the Reformation. But, while adhering to the Roman side on this matter so important to the Eastern Churches, the reformed Churches adhere to the Eastern side in counting the number of Ecumenical Councils! The basis of distinction would seem to be that even a pre-Reformation Council lost its normative quality because the Church had been divided in the much earlier sep-

[11] The first possible reversal is in the proposed form of Eucharist recently issued by the liturgical commission of the Episcopal Church, which omits the *filioque* clause from the Nicene Creed. See *Prayer Book Studies XVII* (New York: The Church Pension Fund, 1967), p. 47. But the new Book of Confessions of the United Presbyterian Church (Philadelphia: Office of the General Assembly, 1966), which was adopted at the General Assembly in Portland in May, 1966, setting forth the Nicene Creed (p. 11) includes the *filioque* even though the footnote calls the text "the first unchallengeably catholic or universal creed deriving from a council of the church" and refers, without qualification, to its use by Eastern Orthodoxy.

aration of the Eastern Churches from the Western.

But the same distinction would apply to earlier Councils: those after the Assyrian Church was out, then those after the Egyptian, Ethiopian and Armenian Churches were out. In fact there is no period in which the Church can be regarded as "undivided." There were always some groups regarded as schismatic and heretical by the majority. Of course the given schismatic groups regarded the majority as heretical; and they regarded *their* Councils and Synods as final and authoritative.

In the Articles of Religion of the Church of England and of its daughter Churches within the Anglican Communion,[12] it is declared (in Article XXI) that "Councils may not be gathered together without the commandment and will of Princes." This requirement in itself would invalidate the later Councils in question but hardly on a tenable theological ground. But Article XXI goes further and declares: "And when they be gathered together, (forasmuch as they be an assembly of men, whereof all be not governed with the Spirit and Word of God,) they may err, and sometimes have erred even in things pertaining unto God." In the American Articles after the heading of Article XXI, *Of the Authority of General Councils*, is set down: "The Twenty-first of the former Articles is omitted; because it is partly of a local and civil nature, and is provided for, as to the remaining parts of it, in other Articles." This makes clear that we did not intend to take a contrary position, namely, affirm the infallibility of the Councils. It is more understandable that, because of the absence the actual negative words found in the English Article are absent, in the American Church there is a frequently expressed assumption that the decrees of the Council have finality. Yet, the same assumption prevails in the Church of England and in the other portions of the Anglican Communion although this fallibilizing reference to the Councils is set out in black and white in every Prayer Book in every pew.

A council of bishops (like any other grouping of persons, all

12 Except for the American Episcopal Church, which in its establishment of the Articles in 1801 omitted these words for obvious reasons.

the way from a nation to a citizens' social action committee) is no more—and no less—than the individuals who make it up. Granted, for convenience of discourse we often speak otherwise; for example, "the First Council of Nicaea decreed . . .," "the National Committee for Peace in Vietnam urged that . . ." But the text of Article XXI is more careful and more realistic: each Council is seen as "an assembly of men" and the fact is expressed that some of the bishops may be "governed by the Spirit and Word of God" and some not. Similar realism is shown in Article XXVIII of the (Lutheran) Augsburg Confession. This text, much longer than the Anglican Article, provides various generic distinctions and particular examples which come down to this: when the decrees of the bishops are in accord with the Gospel (or are sensible and minimal regulations toward order in the Church), then they have authority; otherwise, they do not. The Confession conveniently provides a word from the Lord to support each of the contrasting responses to this ambivalence of authority and lack of authority: "He that heareth you heareth me" (Luke 10:16) as well as "Beware of false prophets" (Matt. 7:15). And in support a bold word from Augustine is used: "Neither must we submit to Catholic bishops if they chance to err, or hold anything contrary to the Canonical Scriptures of God."[13]

What all this comes down to is that if what the bishops decree is true, it's true; if it's not true, it's not. And the determination of what is true or false is made by some other norm than the "authority" being thus judged. The majority vote of individual bishops, however solemnly convened or widespread their representation, simply vanishes as an authority in itself.

The same points are made, but even more sharply, in two fundamental confessions of the Presbyterian-Reformed tradition. The Scots Confession, composed by John Knox and his associates at the request of Parliament in 1560, states that we do not receive uncritically ". . . whatever has been declared to men under the name of the general councils for it is plain that, being

13 *Contra Petiliani Epistolam.*

human, some of them have manifestly erred, and that in matters of great weight and importance."[14] But the full implication is drawn out:

So far then as the council confirms its decrees by the plain Word of God, so far do we reverence and embrace them. But if men, under the name of a council, pretend to forge for us new articles of faith, or to make decisions contrary to the Word of God, then we must utterly deny them as the doctrine of devils, drawing our souls from the voice of the one God to follow the doctrines and teachings of men.[15]

That which is thus rejected is seen as "not the true understanding and meaning of the Holy Ghost, although councils, realms and nations have approved and received it." The three norms for judgment of conciliar decrees are tersely summarized: "We dare not receive or admit any interpretation which is contrary to any principal point of our faith, or to any other plain text of Scripture, or to the rule of love,"[16] and explicitly, as opposed to "any opinion or prerogative that they could not err by reason of their numbers."[17]

The Second Helvetic Confession, the most widely received and adopted Reformed confession during the Reformation period, also makes the point, and quite colorfully:

Wherefore we do not permit ourselves, in controversies about religion or matters of faith, to urge our case with only the opinions of the fathers or decrees of councils; much less by received customs, or by the large number of those who share the same opinion, or by the prescription of a long time. WHO IS THE JUDGE? Therefore, we do not admit any other judge than God himself, who proclaims by the Holy Scriptures what is true, what is false, what is to be followed, or what to be avoided. So we do assent to the judgments of spiritual men which are drawn from the Word of God. Certainly Jeremiah and other prophets vehemently condemned the assemblies

---

[14] *The Scots Confession of 1560,* edited, with introduction, by G. D. Henderson, rendered into modern English by James Bulloch (Edinburgh: St. Andrew Press, 1916), Chap. XX.

[15] *Ibid.*

[16] *Op. cit.,* Chap. XVIII.

[17] *Loc. cit.,* n. 14, above.

of priests which were set up against the law of God; and diligently admonished us that we should not listen to the fathers, or tread in their path who, walking in their own inventions, swerved from the law of God.[18]

But by the time the Long Parliament adopted the Westminster Confession in 1648,[19] a considerably more positive view was taken of Councils. After the positive statement of their purposes, it is declared that "decrees and determinations, if consonant to the Word of God, are to be received with reverence and submission, not only for their agreement with the Word, but also for the power whereby they are made, as being an ordinance of God, appointed thereunto in his Word."[20] Nevertheless, as we read in the next paragraph, "All synods or councils since the apostles' times, whether general or particular, may err, and many have erred; therefore they are not to be made the rule of faith or practice, but to be used as a help in both."

How then in view of the history of these cautionary reservations can we explain the commonly voiced claim, as well as what is often the tacit assumption in many parts of the Christian spectrum, that the doctrinal decrees of a selected number of Councils have finality? A number of reasons may be suggested.

First, at the time of the Reformation the issues with Rome (and in the case of the Westminster Confession, with the Church of England) were quite different from those which occupied the Ecumenical Councils. The Reformers, whether Lutheran, Calvinist, or Anglican, did not critically review these

[18] From *Reform Confessions of the 16th Century*, edited by Arthur C. Cochrane (Philadelphia: Westminster, 1966), Chap. II.

[19] Composed by an Assembly of the Divines convened by the Long Parliament in 1643 and first ratified by the General Assembly of the Church of Scotland in 1647.

[20] *The Humble Advice of the Assembly of Divines, Now by Authority of Parliament Sitting at Westminster, Concerning a Confession of Faith: with the Quotations and Text of Scripture Annexed. Presented by Them Lately to Both Houses of Parliament*, Chap. XXXI. The text in the passages quoted above is that adopted by the United Presbyterian Church in the United States of America in 1958. See *Proposed Book of Confessions* (Philadelphia. Office of the General Assembly, 1966), pp. 150–51.

matters (as is shown, for example, by the unquestioning continuity of even the non-conciliar *filioque* clause). In their various official formularies they simply repeated the old dogmas, either briefly or at length. This they did for three reasons: (a) since each given Confession of Faith purported to be adequate and self-contained, doctrines not at issue had to be covered as well as the new chosen positions; (b) since each reformed Church was claiming to hold correctly the Catholic Faith, it was important to reassure their own members as well as those of other Churches that they were maintaining continuity with as much as possible of the common tradition of doctrine; and (c) there were on the scene at the time of the Reformation individual voices and inchoate sects who were raising challenges more fundamental than those of the classical Reformers, and while it was not felt necessary to engage with them (since they were relatively weak and could be put down by the civil authorities with which each of the reformed Churches was linked), it seemed appropriate to include these taken-for-granted doctrines. *Since, then, doctrinal continuity with the decrees of the Councils was articulated, quite naturally there developed the assumption that the Councils which voted these decrees had authoritative weight.*

Second, until relatively modern times, the Christians of Western culture were out of touch with Churches other than those "Catholic," "Protestant," and "Orthodox," the myth of "the Undivided Church" (presumably from A.D. 33 to 867) was easily indulged in. It was quite natural to assume that what in this "Golden Age" everybody agreed on must be unshakable truth. It is this myth which underlies a maxim which has often been used to buttress the claimed authority not only of the Councils but of more besides, the maxim of St. Vincent of Lérins: *quod semper, quod ubique et ab omnibus;* that is, what has been held always, everywhere, and by all. But as is now more generally known, and has been already spelled out, there never was such a Church; nor was there ever universal acceptance of anything.

Third, we should examine another myth. Especially because

they were held a long time ago in the misty past, there has been attributed to the early Councils a reality transcending the individual episcopal members. While rarely any one in any Church has attributed infallibility to any single bishop (except in the Roman Catholic Church since 1870—and this attribution has been limited to the bishop of only one See), it has nevertheless been assumed that infallibility resided in Councils *per se*. Reflection reveals that to speak of a Council apart from the individuals who composed it presupposes a quite unverifiable ontology. On the other hand, the assertion that the inspiration of the Holy Ghost guarantees the decrees of the Councils to be true raises a host of questions. To mention a few: How could we verify that those bishops who ended up on the minority side in the voting (and were thereafter punished for their pains or continued their "Apostolic Succession" in separate national churches) were less inspired by the Holy Spirit than their confreres? If asked, they would have claimed that the Holy Ghost was on their side. Further, this certainty about the reliable presence of the Holy Ghost is blurred, to say the least, by the plain fact of disagreement between different Communions as to which of the Councils are "Ecumenical." (The Roman Catholic Church accepts 21; the Orthodox Church at some points accepted 8—at other points 7; many Anglicans and Protestants accept 7—though they are not particularly affirmative about the Third (Ephesus, 431), denominating Mary as the Mother of God; the Assyrian Church accepts 2; the Coptic and Armenian Churches accept 3.)

So, to reiterate, what is—on other grounds—seen as true from a Council is accepted while what is not seen as true is not accepted. Therefore, *as such*—just because they are Church Councils—the Councils are not authoritative.

3. *The Creeds*

We now turn to a category of authority which not only calls for independent consideration, but also is useful as a transition between two bases of authority already considered and the three next to be considered. The Creeds used by the Churches that constitute all but a minority of Christians throughout the world are much more conspicuously to the fore as a standard of belief than are any of the other claimed bases of authority. Compared with the other norms they are quite brief; the identical words are used each time; and their public repetition is frequent—weekly, or even daily. As a practical matter, then, the Creeds would seem to serve as the most important working norm.

In this regard the Bible cannot compete. Except for the very active and devoted members of the Fundamentalist sects, Christians as a whole read or hear very little more of the Bible than is read on Sundays in church: short and infrequently repeated passages appointed by fixed lectionaries or reflecting the taste —abiding or transitory—of the minister. As for the decrees of the Ecumenical Councils, very, very few Church members have ever read them.

Further, the Creeds also, in practice (quite apart from theory), outrank in visibility—and audibility—the three norms still to be analyzed. As for the Confessions of Faith of the respective denominations, only a slightly higher percentage of Church members have read them than have studied the decrees of the Councils; and even those who have studied them once do not often refocus their attention on them. A much larger proportion are, of course, in contact with the respective liturgies; but the nature and form of much of this material is such that doctrinal normativeness is not generally suggested. As for consensus—what is actually believed by the members of a given Church—people have always felt a little unsure of their fellow church members in this regard. And increasingly in our times they have had more grounds for this lack of confidence.

This brief comparison of norms—two already analyzed and shown not to provide finality, and three yet to be considered more fully—shows us then why for so many the Creeds operate as the most fundamental norm. Are they sustainable as such?

The three Creeds are commonly known as the Apostles', the

Nicene, and the Athanasian, though the attribution of none of these titles is correct. They all appear to have originated or reached their present form in about the same period—the fourth and fifth centuries.

The only creedal material to receive official adoption by a Council is a considerable portion of what is now called the "Nicene Creed"; the form which was adopted at Nicaea (325) is by no means identical with the text as it is now known and used. The principal difference is that in place of the present last portion which contains many statements there are simply these words: "And in the Holy Spirit"—followed by four anathemas against Arianism which for a while were treated as an integral part of the text. Also, our present form of this Creed contains words from another declaration, referred to as the Nicaeo-Constantinopolitan Creed,[21] which included more material on a definition of the Person of Jesus but lacked the phrase "from the substance of the Father," which appeared in the original Nicene Creed. It also included a more involved statement about the nature and workings of the Holy Ghost and brief assertions of belief in the Church, Baptism, the resurrection of the dead and eternal life—all of this now encompassed in what we call the "Nicene Creed." Happily the anathemas which concluded the original Nicene Creed were omitted. In the fifth century the Eastern Church, beginning with Antioch, began to use this composite as the affirmation of faith in Baptism. Gradually this Creed began to be added to the eucharistic liturgy in both the East and the West—where later the *filioque* was added.

The Apostles' Creed is limited to the Western Church. An eighth-century writer is the first to quote it in its present form, but something like the present Apostles' Creed was used in Rome and other Western Churches by the fourth century, and a legend developed that it was jointly composed by the twelve Apostles. It began to be used in Baptism in the Western Churches as the

21 It is now recognized that there is no convincing basis for connecting it with the First Council of Constantinople (381), which until recently was generally claimed to be the authority for it.

Nicene Creed had been used in the Eastern Churches.[22] It is shorter than the Nicene Creed in its affirmations about each of the three Persons of the Trinity. It differs in the closing list of doctrines in that it puts, in place of the Nicene "the resurrection of the dead," an affirmation of a particular view of the mode of this process: known as *resurrectio carnis,* "the resurrection of the flesh," which is softened somewhat in the English translation by the use of the words "the resurrection of the body."

The Athanasian Creed, also known as *Quicunque Vult* (from the opening Latin words), appeared in the Western Church, receiving limited adoption in the Eastern Church only from the eighteenth century. It obviously was not composed by St. Athanasius since it contains doctrinal expressions that arose from controversies developing after his time and also since it was composed in Latin and not in Greek. Many feel that it may have been written by St. Ambrose, Bishop of Milan. The version that appears in the English Book of Common Prayer suffers from some mistranslations and, further, the reformers based their rendering on inaccurate texts. But, as is pointed out by Canon F. L. Cross, sometime Lady Margaret Professor of Divinity at Oxford, "in the present circumstances any alteration would give the impression that something of the traditional faith was being surrendered."[23] Since those establishing the American Episcopal Church refused to include this Creed, and since it has dropped out of use in virtually all Protestant Churches, and since it is not used in the Roman Catholic Church parish worship but only on the occasion of the monastic and clergy office of Prime, it is unfamiliar to most members. Hence, examples will be given to show its general tenor (as it consists of forty-two declarations it is too long to set forth in full).

22 This traditional usage no longer obtains in the Anglican and certain other reformed Churches.

23 *The Oxford Dictionary of the Christian Church* (London: Oxford University Press, 1957), p. 99. In the Church of England and some other parts of the Anglican Communion, the Athanasian Creed is required to be sung or read at Matins on thirteen holy days.

It opens and closes with anathemas, such as in the introduction: "Whosoever will be saved before all things it is necessary that he hold the Catholic Faith. Which faith except everyone do keep whole and undefiled, without doubt he shall perish everlastingly." On the Trinity there are such definitions as: "Neither confounding the Persons: nor dividing the Substance"; ". . . not three incomprehensibles, nor three uncreated: but one uncreated and one incomprehensible"; "the Son is of the Father alone: not made nor created, but begotten"; "the Holy Ghost is of the Father, and of the Son: neither made nor created, nor begotten, but proceeding." "He, therefore, that will be saved: must thus think of the Trinity." On Jesus: "God of the Substance of the Father, . . . and Man of the Substance of his Mother . . . of a reasonable soul and human flesh subsisting"; "One, not by conversion of the Godhead into flesh: but by taking of the Manhood into God"; "One altogether, not by confusion of Substance: but by unity of Person."

The first thing to be observed is that all three of the Creeds emerged in approximately the same period and no one of them, as such, received adoption by the corporate action of the Church. If the authoritative basis for them is to be antiquity, there is no basis for not accepting all three as absolute if any one of them is to be required as a final criterion for belief. Yet as has been pointed out, the new American Episcopal Church at its formation rejected both the Athanasian Creed and the Nicene Creed, only reluctantly restoring the latter as a result of a compromise made with the Archbishop of Canterbury as the price for securing the English episcopal succession.[24] The United Presbyterian Church in the United States of America has just currently, in the official adoption of its Book of Confessions, included the Nicene Creed, but in doing so grounded the text in the First Council of Con-

[24] E. Clowes Chorley, *Men and Movements in the American Episcopal Church* (New York: Scribner's, 1946), p. 139; W. W. Manross, *A History of the American Episcopal Church*, 3d ed., rev. (New York: Morehouse-Barlow, 1959), pp. 189 ff.; "The American Church Becomes Independent," Chap. 3 in Henry Thompson Malone, *The Episcopal Church in Georgia* (Atlanta: The Protestant Episcopal Church in the Diocese of Atlanta, 1960), pp. 39 ff.

stantinople,[25] *filioque* clause and all. Though at the Reformation
the reformers accepted the Athanasian Creed, none of the successor Churches in this country has accepted it, and most
Protestant Churches do not use the Nicene Creed. These various
desuetudes somewhat blur resort to antiquity as an authoritative
basis for assuming the finality of the Creeds. In any case the
early Church did not have them, and it would be difficult to find
a logical basis for determining that the fifth century has a special
finality (as distinguished from the centuries preceding it, and
the centuries since the Reformation).

Insofar as a large portion of the Nicene Creed was in fact
decreed by the First Council of Nicaea, whatever claim of
finality this affords depends upon one's being able to attribute
infallibility to Councils. And, as we have seen, there are a number of reasons why one cannot. In fact, the Confessions of Faith
of principal Churches definitely do not so dignify the Councils.[26]
Affirmations do not necessarily have any greater finality than
have the councils which have decreed them.

A further difficulty has arisen since the time of Copernicus.
Before his "heretical" view that the earth is round, it was generally believed that there was a three-layer universe with Heaven
above and Hell beneath. Granted, it has taken theology and
homiletics a long time to catch up with the Copernican world
view accepted by everybody in every other field of thought; nevertheless, today many spokesmen have felt it necessary to demythologize the phrases in the Creeds which have directional
references. And with the present-day openness to alternatives
about the form of personal life after death, the phrase that is
authentically *resurrectio carnis* has been demythologized. Having gone soft with regard to absoluteness in these respects,
"orthodox" churchmen have lost any basis (although few of
them have become aware of this fact)[27] for objecting to further

[25] But see p. 60, and n. 2, above.
[26] See pp. 53–56, above.
[27] For example, the chief accuser of the author, who in his draft presentment for heresy cited the latter's nonaffirmation of the Virgin Birth
as failing in conformity to the Creeds, in a sermon in the principal

creedal demythologization (for example: as to "conceived by the Holy Ghost, born of the Virgin Mary"). As far as *authority* goes, logic counsels "all or nothing."

This selective nonacceptance, or "fuzzing up," of Articles of the Creed necessarily implies the use of some more basic yardstick, other than the Creeds; hence the Creeds as such lose their validity as binding authority. The English Articles of Religion[28] point to a more basic norm. In asserting that they "ought thoroughly (sic) to be received and believed," this basis is given: "for they may be proved by most certain warrants of Holy Scripture." There are two difficulties with this basis of authority for the Creeds. First, the bulk of the Athanasian Creed has no parallel in scriptural language, forms of thought, or teaching. This is true of a key phrase from the Nicene Creed "being of one substance with the Father"—as was consistently pointed out by those at Nicaea who were opposed to the adoption of this phrase in the first place. Second, as we have seen, the Scriptures themselves can in no wise be seen as a final norm: what is true in them is accepted and what is not, is not—and this presupposes some yardstick outside of the Scriptures themselves for making this selection.

In the American Episcopal Church there has been a tendency to support the Creeds on the basis that they are part of the Prayer Book. From this approach which we lawyers call *nunc pro tunc* (literally "now for then"),[29] one would think we Angli-

---

Episcopal Church in Wheeling, on the day of the opening of the House of Bishops' meeting where the matter of heresy presentment was to be under consideration, himself soundly demythologized three of the creedal affirmations.

[28] VIII. *Of the Three Creeds.* The American form of the Articles already displays an exercise of discrimination (and thus displays an unspoken outside norm), omitting the word "three" and in the text omitting reference to the Athanasian Creed.

[29] In the judicial opinions in the only two cases of deposition for heresy in our century (the Rev. Dr. Algernon S. Crapsey in 1907, and Bishop William Montgomery Brown in 1924), neither the Bible nor the Articles of Religion were resorted to as norms; rather, the major premise in the syllogism of judgment was the Prayer Book: on this basis the Creeds were relevant.

cans had invented the Creeds! To the degree that such a quixotic view of church history can be taken seriously, there would have to be assumed the finality of the Prayer Book. As to how supportable such a claim is we shall see shortly.

Also, commonly resorted to for bolstering up the Creeds is the argument from consensus; a recent example is found in a footnote to the Nicene Creed in the Presbyterian Book of Confessions already referred to: "unchallengeably catholic or universal."[30] How solid such consensus is we shall also shortly examine.

However authoritative these other bases may or may not be held to be, what clearly comes through is the fact that the Creeds do not stand on their own feet as a basis of authority. And if one or another did, it would require some basic norm to decide that one or two are to be so accepted, and one or two not accepted, since none of them is found in the primitive Church, all arose in the same later period, and none *in toto* came into being by official conciliar decree.

4. *Liturgies*

It is here we find the greatest variation, both as between Christian communions and within any one of the communions at different historical periods. This can be approached, both as a matter of principle and as a matter of fact. Practically every Confession of Faith asserts the variability and relativity of such forms (for example: "Every particular or national Church hath authority to ordain, change and abolish, Ceremonies or Rites of the Church ordained only by man's authority, so that all things be done to edifying"[31]). This has been consistently acted out in the various Churches. To be specific, and timely, the American Episcopal Prayer Book has been in the process of revision for some years.[32] Right now under study in the Church is a radically

[30] See n. 20, above. The footnotes in the Book of Confessions are, however, not an official part thereof (*op. cit.*, Preface).

[31] *Articles of Religion*, Article XXXIV.

[32] The same is true of other portions of the Anglican Communion, with considerably changed versions having been adopted in many countries.

different form of the Eucharist which could be presented to the forthcoming General Convention for adoption for trial use, and the changes are not only linguistic, structural, or choreographic. For example, in the Prayer of Consecration the substitutionary ("pay off") doctrine of the Atonement is eliminated and, as has been pointed out, the *filioque* clause has been omitted from the Creed.

The very fact that liturgies can be overhauled—and, happily, are being—makes clear that they have no finality and that some superior norm or norms are involved in the process of formulating changes. Granted, this has not always been perceived. In a television interview at Wheeling, the Bishop of South Florida affirmed the ultimacy of the Prayer Book, and then when reminded that it is under revision, declared that were that already accomplished he would attribute finality to the revised Prayer Book. This is in effect a nihilism as far as a perennial basis of belief is concerned: translated, it means "whatever is, is."

A mere look at various items in the present Prayer Book would require nonaffirmation or doubt on the part of the average sensible person;[33] but in fairness to intelligent people (like one bishop just referred to) in my Communion who use round

---

and with a new form of Eucharist currently under debate in the mother church's Church Assembly.

[33] For example, (1) the Collect for Holy Innocents Day: "O Almighty God, who out of the mouths of babes and sucklings hast ordained strength, and madest infants to glorify thee by their deaths; Mortify and kill all vices in us, and so strengthen us by thy grace, that by the innocency of our lives, and constancy of our faith even unto death, we may glorify thy holy Name; through Jesus Christ our Lord" (p. 102).

(2) The first Collect for the Communion of the Sick: "Almighty, everliving God, Maker of mankind, who dost correct those whom thou dost love, and chastise every one whom thou dost receive; We beseech thee to have mercy upon this thy servant visited with thine hand, and to grant that he may take his sickness patiently, and recover his bodily health, if it be thy gracious will; and that, whensoever his soul shall depart from the body, it may be without spot presented unto thee; through Jesus Christ our Lord." (p. 321).

(3) The phrase in the devotionally moving Prayer of Humble Access embodying an unfounded medieval superstitious distinction: ". . . so to

phrases like "the Faith of the Prayer Book" or "loyalty to the Prayer Book" or who designate themselves as "Prayer Book Catholics," what they really mean is that they give assent or faith to what is actually a selection of statements which to them seem to be basic therein, and to what is felt, without too much precision, to be the general drift of the book's contents. Many such Churchmen, when confronted with this portion or that, readily enough express disbelief, doubt, or diffidence. But perhaps not fully enough appreciated by them, or by others, is the fact that implicit in this fairly widespread approach is that some other norm (apart from the Prayer Book itself) is consciously or unconsciously in operation. Hence, in itself, neither this nor any other denominational form of worship can serve as a final authority for belief.

5. *Confessions of Faith*

Reference has already been made, in the consideration of other norms, to various official declarations adopted by particular denominations at given points in their history. Some of these are very lengthy and detailed; some are relatively brief. Virtually none of them is irenic in spirit or language; but some are more hostile in tone to other Christian groups than others are. The principal declarations explicitly undermine any claim to finality on the part of the official gatherings in the early Church[34]—ones at least as authoritative as the convocations which adopted the given Confessions and certainly more representative in geographical extent. Yet generally lacking in the text of these Confessions, which boldly declare the human fallibility of the Ecumenical Councils, is any recognition of the same characteristic in their own functioning.

Indisputable, for example, is Anglican Article XIX: "As the Church of Jerusalem, Alexandria, and Antioch have erred; so also the Church of Rome hath erred, not only in their living and

---

eat the flesh of thy dear Son Jesus Christ, and to drink his blood, that our sinful *bodies* may be made clean by his *body,* and our *souls* washed through his most precious *blood.* . . ." (p. 82; italics supplied).

[34] See pp. 53–58, above.

manner of Ceremonies, but also in matters of Faith"—as far as it goes, But to complete the thought is needed just six more words: "so also hath the Church of England."

Just this year has been adopted by a major Christian body a Confession which is virtually unique in Christian history in that in its very Preface it recognizes not only the positive value and relative character of the previous Confessions, but also its *own* limitations. The Confession of 1967 of the United Presbyterian Church in the United States of America has many merits, not the least these words, very much worth quoting at some length, from its Preface:

> The church confesses its faith when it bears a present witness to God's grace in Jesus Christ.
>
> In every age the church has expressed its witness in words and deeds as the need of the time required. The earliest examples of confession are found within the Scriptures. Confessional statements have taken such varied forms as hymns, liturgical formulas, doctrinal definitions, catechisms, theological systems in summary, and declarations of purpose against threatening evil.
>
> Confessions and declarations are subordinate standards in the church, subject to the authority of Jesus Christ, the Word of God, as the Scriptures bear witness to him. No one type of confession is exclusively valid, no one statement is irreformable. Obedience to Jesus Christ alone identifies the one universal church and supplies the continuity of its tradition. This obedience is the ground of the church's duty and freedom to reform itself in life and doctrine as new occasions, in God's providence, may demand.
>
> The United Presbyterian Church in the United States of America acknowledges itself aided in understanding the gospel by the testimony of the church from earlier ages and from many lands.[35]

6. *Consensus*

What has been assumed to be the general agreement of believers has often served as support for doctrines. Sometimes this is

[35] *Op. cit* (n. 20, above), p. 177. The word "virtually" in the opening sentence of the paragraph introducing the above quotation is meant to take account of the fact that a similar spirit is reflected in the Scots' Confession of 1560 (see n. 14).

stated explicitly, as for example in the time-honored phrase *consensus fidelium* and in the "Canon" (i.e., "rule") of St. Vincent of Lérins already referred to. Looking at it simply from a "natural" basis, the fact of a universal conviction about something would hardly seem to be probative. History is too full of instances where virtually everybody was wrong, and the truth (as subsequently established and accepted) lay with a "majority of one." But proponents of consensus sometimes claim a difference because of a "supernatural" factor: the operation of the Holy Spirit. But there is no way to provide independent verification for this assumption, and, further, the assumption makes it difficult to explain conflicting views held on the same doctrinal issues in different periods of church history. For example, compare the almost universally held view of the first Christians that Jesus was subordinate to the Father, with the later almost universal denial of His subordination.

In addition to these logical difficulties, there is a factual aspect about which now it is possible to deal on a basis of definite data.

During most of the centuries of the Church's life, civil and criminal sanctions were available to enforce conformity. Thus few Church members were brave enough to indicate that they actually did not accept official doctrinal positions. As in country after country these sanctions were removed, there still remained strong social sanctions which considerably constricted any widespread expression of skepticism. In what has become a more "open" society, more and more Church members have become open about their doubts and dissents; but since until recently there have been no data by way of statistical studies, it still has been widely assumed that "practically all" members of each Church believe its teachings.

We are now in a time, however, when this matter need not be left to mere speculation. Surveys utilizing the scientific method are becoming available which reveal what Church members actually do believe. The one with the widest coverage and depth is that under the direction of Professor Charles Y. Glock and Dr. Rodney Stark, and undertaken by the Survey Research Center at the University of California at Berkeley.[36]

A few samples of the results of this survey will be sufficient to focus the problem.

For the rather basic affirmation, "I know God really exists and I have no doubts about it," the positive replies were: Congregationalists, 41 per cent[37]; Methodists, 60 per cent; Episcopalians, 63 per cent; Disciples of Christ, 76 per cent; United Presbyterians, 75 per cent; Lutherans, 73 per cent;[38] American (Northern) Baptists, 78 per cent; Lutherans–Missouri Synod, 81 per cent. Southern Baptists, 99 per cent; Roman Catholics, 81 per cent.[39] For the statement, "Jesus is the Divine Son of God and I have no doubts about it," the results were: Congregationalists, 40 per cent; Methodists, 54 per cent; Episcopalians, 59 per cent; Disciples, 74 per cent; United Presbyterians, 72 per cent; Lutherans, 74 per cent; American Baptists, 76 per cent; Lutherans —Missouri Synod, 93 per cent; Southern Baptists, 99 per cent; Roman Catholics, 86 per cent. Again, others were able to say Yes to less affirmative statements. As to acceptance of "Jesus was born of a Virgin," most of the percentages were even lower: Congregationalists, 21 per cent; Methodists, 34 per cent; Episcopalians, 39 per cent; Disciples of Christ, 62 per cent; United Presbyterians, 57 per cent; Lutherans, 66 per cent; American Baptists, 69 per cent; Lutherans–Missouri Synod, 92 per cent;

36 Several volumes based on the material have been published: *Religion and Society in Tension* (Chicago: Rand, McNally & Co., 1965); *Christian Beliefs and Anti-Semitism* (New York: Harper & Row, 1966)—both by Dr. Glock and Dr. Stark, *To Comfort and To Challenge* (Berkeley and Los Angeles: University of California Press, 1967), by Dr. Glock, Benjamin Ringer, and Earl R. Babbie. Published also has been a survey by the latter of the views of the women of the Episcopal Diocese of California (San Francisco: *The Pacific Churchman*, January, 1967, pp. 1 f.).

37 In the course of the study the Congregational Christian Churches united with the Evangelical and Reformed Church to form the United Church of Christ.

38 Including the Lutheran Church of America and the American Lutheran Church. For the sake of brevity "Lutheran" will be used for them in what follows, with full recognition that those of the Missouri Synod, separately categorized, are equally authentic Lutherans!

39 A certain percentage in each case were able to say Yes to "While I have doubts, I feel that I do believe in God" and to other less affirmative statements.

Southern Baptists, 99 per cent; Roman Catholics, 81 per cent. The percentages of affirmation of the assertion "Jesus walked on water" is low for most churches. This is not surprising in light of the percentages of those who believe that it is absolutely necessary to hold "the Bible to be God's truth": Congregationalists, 23 per cent; Methodists, 39 per cent; Episcopalians, 32 per cent; Disciples, 58 per cent; United Presbyterians, 52 per cent; Lutherans, 64 per cent; American Baptists, 58 per cent; Lutherans —Missouri Synod, 80 per cent; Southern Baptists, 61 per cent; Roman Catholics, 38 per cent.

In the light of the victory in the early Church of the eschatalogical alternative (see pp. 46-47), interesting are the replies to the question, "Do you believe Jesus will actually return to the earth some day?" The percentages of those answering "definitely" are as follows: Congregationalists, 13 per cent; Methodists, 21 per cent; Episcopalians, 24 per cent; Disciples, 36 per cent; United Presbyterians, 43 per cent; Lutherans, 54 per cent; American Baptists, 57 per cent; Lutherans—Missouri Synod, 75 per cent; Southern Baptists, 94 per cent; Roman Catholics, 47 per cent. It is interesting that in response to the alternatives of "probably"/"possibly," considerably more answered the latter than the former (e.g., only 8 per cent of Congregationalists, 12 per cent of Methodists and 13 per cent of Episcopalians found the notion "probable," though a somewhat larger minority were willing to say that it is "possible").

On the affirmation of life beyond death, those in the "probable" category are higher than in the case of the Second Coming and the same is true of those answering "completely true": 36 per cent for Congregationalists; 49 per cent for Methodists; 53 per cent for Episcopalians and 75 per cent for Roman Catholics. Very much lower are the percentages of those responding positively on the existence of the Devil and on the classical doctrine of Original Sin. In the case of the latter, the following are the percentages: Congregationalists, 2 per cent; Methodists, 7 per cent; Episcopalians, 18 per cent; Disciples, 6 per cent; United Presbyterians, 21 per cent; Lutherans, 49 per cent; American Baptists, 23 per cent; Lutherans—Missouri Synod, 86 per cent; Southern Baptists, 43 percent; Roman Catholics, 68 per cent.

Higher but not impressively so are the number of those believing that belief in Jesus Christ as Savior is absolutely necessary for salvation: Congregationalists, 38 per cent; Methodists, 45 per cent; Episcopalians, 47 per cent; Disciples, 78 per cent; United Presbyterians, 66 per cent; Lutherans, 77 per cent; American Baptists, 78 per cent; Lutherans–Missouri Synod, 97 per cent; Southern Baptists, 97 per cent; Roman Catholics, 51 per cent. Connected with the doctrine of sole salvation through Jesus Christ has been the teaching as to the necessity of Baptism for salvation.[40] But the degree of credence given the traditional claim is only 11 per cent among Congregationalists; 19 per cent among Methodists; 39 per cent among Episcopalians, and 28 per cent among Presbyterians, and only 19 per cent among Southern Baptists.

Complete logical consistency in theological belief is not displayed by this survey or by others. A rather comprehensive Gallup Poll made in England in 1965 showed that just fewer than one half of the members of the Church of England believed in a personal God; but that two thirds believed that Jesus is the Son of God—reminding one of what is said to be the conviction of many Latin Americans: there is no God, but Mary is His Mother!

To recapitulate: It is obvious that as a matter of logic consensus—assuming the factuality of this concept—cannot provide a reliable test of truth, theological or otherwise. But now we see that, as a matter of fact, not a great deal of consensus can be found in the Christian fold, not even on beliefs officially taught. In addition to the obvious lack of consensus across the board, there is marked lack of consensus within most of the principal denominations.

[40] For example, the Ministration of Holy Baptism, Book of Common Prayer, page 273: "None can enter into the Kingdom of God except he be regenerate and born anew of Water and of the Holy Ghost" (based on John 3:3, 5).

Recognition of this fact should somewhat relieve the minds of certain leaders in the more "liberal" Churches during this period in which there are more and more exponents in the seminaries and among the clergy of what is given the catch-all title, the "New Theology." A number of ecclesiastical officials (including some whose ballots would have been cast on the No side of a good many of the statements referred to above) have been displaying considerable nervousness about disturbance of "the little people." Without the benefit of having reviewed the various available surveys, and in the modern day complication of ecclesiastical administration perhaps not very much in touch with the range of actual views of the laity, they have been known to deem it "irresponsible" and "lacking in pastoral sensitivity" for clergy to speak openly and honestly on a basis of their study of the questions and to reveal to the laity their doubts and nonaffirmations.

For example, in my own Church, it would appear from the survey drawn from above (and its conclusions are in general validated not only by the reliable methodology adhered to by the staff, but also—though less precisely of course—by many candid statements of laymen by correspondence and in person) that 61 per cent of Episcopal laymen cannot affirm as historical the Virgin Birth and 53 per cent will not affirm the doctrine of sole salvation through Jesus—just to take as samples two Prayer Book doctrines for nonaffirmation of which I am at present the defendant in pending heresy proceedings. Mention of the latter fact can help sharpen an important point: the fact that an impressive majority of members of the Church believe (or, more accurately, disbelieve) as I do does *not*, as such, establish that I am right, or even that I am not heretical. But figures such as these do give substance to a sense of responsibility and pastoral sensitivity which many of us feel toward what is shown to be the majority of Church members: by our own candor to relieve them somewhat of their growing sense of hypocrisy as the credibility gap is fast widening between unqualified Prayer Book statements and what seems to them plausible.

Part of a bishop's promise at his own consecration is to be "ready, with all faithful diligence, to banish and drive away from the Church all erroneous and strange doctrines." Each of these adjectives bears a different relationship to the type of data we have just been considering. It is evident that doctrines like the ones last mentioned (and all the more so with something like the Second Coming) are becoming stranger and stranger to Episcopalians—not to mention the increasing number of un-churched. But as to whether they are "erroneous," consensus is not relevant. Nor is it relevant in determining the meaning of the word "doctrine" in the Oath of Conformity included in the same Consecration service. Consensus is no more a basis of finality than are the Bible, the Ecumenical Councils, the Creeds, liturgies, or denominational Confessions of Faith.

CHAPTER V

FACTS + FAITH

Wherever one goes and listens to the ever-rising chorus of voices denying or questioning this or that doctrine of Christianity (or criticizing the Church as an institution) there is one recurring question, stated in one form or another: What can a man believe?

Up to this point we have been considering How can a man believe? An attempt has been made to show why no answer can be given to this question on any kind of an authority basis. (It has been suggested that any authority lacks supportable grounding, and this conclusion has been reached by two routes —analytical and descriptive.)

Logic and history both reveal the relative character of any of the conventional bases of authority. At the same time, fewer and fewer thinking people are in fact accepting dogmas so based.

The positive answer to the question, How can a man believe? has been implied in all that has been said up to this point. A man can believe what is shown to emerge from the application of the very process that he uses in his workaday existence—the *empirical method*. This method, in brief, consists of

a. Examination of relevant data,
b. The drawing of a plausible inference from the data,

c. Affirmation of the consequent hypothesis by faith, and

d. Action based on this faith-affirmation.

Can any recognizably Christian conclusions be reached by this method? Or, to put it more broadly, can any religious truth emerge from this process? One thing seems fairly clear. None can be derived, plausibly, by any *other* method.

To put the matter descriptively, less and less will people believe conclusions reached by any other route. The only avenue open now is the faith-affirmation based on empirical data. But before proceeding to specific analyses that will test the validity of the method itself, two precautions against unnecessary disappointment in the results should be stated at the outset.

First, no matter how solid are the data examined or how wide the scope of data available, a given meaning-affirmation is not *entailed* by the data—that is, compelled by it. To affirm is to take a "leap of faith," to use Søren Kierkegaard's phrase. This act of faith will be a personal commitment to a plausible inference based on data. Such a leap of faith carries some of the same quality as the act of faith one gives to conclusions based on a foundation of authority. Still, there is a difference: grounded in data, the affirmation is likely to be a more modest one. There is, in such affirmations, a built-in resistance to extrapolation right up to the skies, to *over-belief*.

However, the fact of the existence of this element of faith does not mean that the method no longer fits the category "empirical." Count, weigh, and measure identical items (as in a physics laboratory or in a mathematical problem), and little or no faith is needed to draw a conclusion. However, as one goes up the scale of complexity and differentiation in the things being counted, through the upper reaches of the life sciences and into the social sciences, the degree of "faith-leap" needed to draw conclusions increases accordingly.

An example of this increasing complexity is afforded by recent studies of the relationship of church commitment to socio-ethical attitudes.[1] These studies proceeded on a scientific basis, but in

[1] See p. 69, n. 36, above.

listing the social views of a wide spread of individuals, and putting them into a pattern useful for analysis under generic headings, a degree of imprecision creeps in. (Take, for example, the measurement of the degree of orthodoxy. This classification is based on the number of doctrines believed. Yet the question of just how each person actually receives given doctrines illustrates how wide a variation is possible between individuals.)

The particular doctrines chosen for the testing of such a sample vary considerably in relative importance both abstractly and for the given individual. On the other side of the comparison (socio-ethical attitudes) there is considerable variation in the intensity and zeal with which views are held—or opposed. Nevertheless, because the over-all differentials are quite marked, one can plausibly draw conclusions.

Taken *in toto*, the data suggest that there is an inverse correlation between the depth of church involvement and Christian social ethics; but, in so concluding, even with all these data at hand, more of a leap of faith is needed than would be required in conclusions drawn from a survey of animal behavior. (And such a study takes more faith in reaching conclusions than does physics.)

Hence it does not seem surprising that conclusions drawn as to *ultimate* meaning involve an even greater leap of faith, regardless of the soundness of the extent of the data on which the conclusions are based.

Second, the more overarching the conclusion, the broader the data base should be. Also, one must be somewhat wary about what is or is not "fact." In the physical sciences, for example, data are limited to visible items or phenomena that can be objectively studied. Likewise, in paleontological and archaeological studies conclusions are drawn from a base supported by the tangible objects found in various "digs," and dated by such things as radioactive carbon tests.

In both examples, hypotheses are inferred, based on the facts, visible objects, and tangible measurements accessible to all who choose to retrace the steps of the original scientists.

Similarly, in the field of cosmogeny, the basic data consist of visible or discernible astronomical bodies whose presence and movement can be detected and measured by radio-electronic means. (Even here the cosmic conclusions drawn are not entailed in the data, as is demonstrated by the co-existence of two opposed notions about the origins of the universe, the "big bang" theory and the "steady state" theory.)

When sociological studies (and particularly those involving attitudes) come under consideration, the scope of "fact" becomes somewhat more extended. Taken into account is a combination of the external behavior of a person and his own statements about his motivation. Balancing one with the other, the behavioral scientists frequently recognize that the only real sources of information about behavior and attitudes that govern behavior are the subjects' statements about it.

An interesting example is the well known study of sexual behavior under the direction of the late Dr. Alfred L. Kinsey.[2] In such a study, obviously there would have been difficulties in acquiring the data directly.

The team that produced these works would be the first to admit that entire credibility cannot be given to the statements of each person interviewed. A basis for general conclusions is achieved by the breadth of the empirical base and by the assumption of margins of error and/or the counterbalancing of two margins of error (e.g., those overly modest in answering questions about their sexual activity and those tending to exaggerate).

By contrast, in recent studies of quite a different type, Dr. William H. Masters, Dr. Virginia E. Johnson and their staff sought to narrow this gap between personal reporting and the actual mechanical facts in sexual activity and response.[3] The sexual activity was staged in a laboratory extensively equipped

[2] *Sexual Behavior in the Human Male* (Bloomington: Indiana University Press, 1951); *Sexual Behavior in the Human Female* (Indiana University Press, 1953).

[3] See their *Human Sexual Response* (Boston: Little, Brown, and Co., 1966).

with surveillance equipment and measuring devices. While these studies gave greater precision and a more solid factual basis for medical conclusions drawn about physiological effects of sexual functioning, they do not correspond too precisely to unobserved and less self-conscious sexual behavior.

This contrast is not meant to value one study over the other. The point is that certain types of conclusions can rest on objectively verifiable data that others may observe (through the study of the resulting electrocardiograms, motion pictures, etc.), while other useful conclusions with a different scope are derived from the less precise interview methods.

When we turn to analyses of psychological patterns, based on a wide variety of individual cases, similar subtleties present themselves. There may be a fund of external data (physiological information, behavior patterns and observable environmental conditions), yet sound conclusions would be difficult indeed to attain if people were not invited to describe their internal states in interviews.

Obviously there is a possible margin of error here, not only in general, but in each instance. In no case could it be positively asserted that what is articulated is *identical* with what precisely has been experienced by a particular subject. What gives a fairly reliable character to generics abstracted from the mass of data is the quantity of persons and experiences included in the survey. The lack of even quality is made up by quantity; yet the quantum of the inferring is considerable.

The fact that an element of inference is added to the body of facts to facilitate a conclusion has put no reins on the progress of research. Nor has there been notable hesitancy to take deliberate action based on a "faith-leap," on a composite of fact and faith.

Yet the negative side of the employment of faith should be stated, also. As has been seen, field after field depends on extrapolation beyond what is strictly compelled by the data themselves. The greater such extrapolation, the more conclusions based on it become informed guesses and the less they retain high probability. At some point, the informed guess verges into the outright gamble. Gamblers may enjoy their diversions, but their methods clearly are not suited to such fields as structural design, medical diagnosis, branch-banking, or freeway route-surveying.

Recognition that inference is involved in varying degrees in various fields does not perforce imply a willingness to extrapolate all the way to the skies. A degree of modesty where conclusions are being drawn is appropriate. A similar attitude needs to be carefully observed in the field of religion as well, if religious beliefs are to have the ring of credibility in our empirical age.

In no scientific discipline does one simply observe and report whatever facts happen to drift into one's purview, willy-nilly. If this were the prevalent method of empirical science, the inference of generics would be a rare event.

Things move in a different direction. There is a focusing on one or more subjects of inquiry. Then there is a narrowing down —and finally, isolation—of data which, under a working hypothesis, could, if verified, form a basis for a conclusion. Such an approach is no less appropriate in the effort to apply the empirical method in the hope of making sound faith-affirmations about the larger meanings of life and reality.

In the histories of religions, many, many questions have been asked and as many answers have been offered—however reached, or whatever their relative importance. What, now and perennially, are the most significant questions? Among them certainly are these:

1. What is it really to be a person?
2. Is death the end?
3. What is the whole universe about?

Men in past centuries, more amenable to and conditioned by the structures of religious authorities, would have been more likely to focus on these questions in the reverse order; but with the widespread secularization of life and thought, these questions are more often voiced today in the order listed above. This, roughly, is in degree of existential awareness.

It seems entirely consistent that this order of inquiry is also more appropriate to the empirical method, beginning with that which is more commonly experienced and experienceable here and now.

CHAPTER VI

THE STYLE OF LIFE

The *ought* cannot be derived from the *is* by the process of reasoning, no matter how complete one's knowledge of the facts. This is evidenced by the fact that intelligent men of good will can on specific questions come out with radically opposed views toward implications of the same data for ethics and for moral action. What makes this difference is the presence in their minds of convictions about meaning and purpose. These convictions may rest on some fixed authority—for example, authorities of the types analyzed in Chapter IV, or others; or they may have been reached—soundly or unsoundly—by making what appear to be plausible inferences. These inferences may have been made from a limited or a broad empirical base, but in either case, reaching the conviction involved making a leap of faith, small or great.

Whenever this second method, that of inference, has been followed, it is obvious that facts have had a causative effect in what makes up the conclusion. However, in the case of convictions which have a "pre-fab" authority base, facts well may have had no part in the matter at all, and for working purposes may be deemed irrelevant.

For example: Among the many correlations provided in the

reports of the studies of Dr. Alfred Kinsey and his colleagues at the University of Indiana is the indication that married women who have had pre-marital sexual experience are more likely to have a successful pattern of sexual fulfillment after marriage. For one whose philosophy of morality is Code ethics, knowledge of these data would have no bearing on his conviction regarding pre-marital sex for it would be negative in any case for him. But, for one whose moral outlook takes the pattern of situation ethics, knowledge of such facts and the generic drawn from them would be relevant. However, they would not be conclusive in providing an endorsement for pre-marital sex—either in general or in a particular case. For him to be consistent in his situational approach there would need to be a number of other factors (supported either by other types of data or by experience —personal or vicarious) which he would weigh in drawing a conclusion.

To sharpen the point, let us assume that available to the Code ethicist and to the situationist are precisely the same body of facts, and that identical is the degree of acceptance of the surveyor's generic summary. In one case, any possible relevance of all this to the drawing of a moral conclusion is automatically foreclosed by the higher priority of adherence to an absolute ethical norm. In the other case the facts are relevant and worthy of consideration, though they would not of themselves be conclusive in providing a Yes or No answer to the particular ethical question. But it is important to stress that to whatever degree the data used in the example have a place in the process of reaching the conclusion, no amount of facts *alone* account for the conclusion. Only by making an inference, a leap of faith, can an "ought" be derived.

The same alternative approaches apply to the process of making a more comprehensive affirmation about the style of life appropriate to man.

Authorities of the type we discussed earlier in connection with other over-all meaning-affirmations offer—sometimes imperiously—only a few ready-made conclusions about man's role and fulfillment. The classical *Creeds* are completely silent in this regard.[1] Similarly, the decrees of the *Councils* are barren of norms for the living of human life. Some of the *Confessions* provide something of a general pattern[2] and the motivation behind it, and the various official catechisms issued at the time of the Reformation provided somewhat more specific norms for conduct.[3]

[1] But at least one official statement of faith is not silent, that of the United Church of Christ:

He calls us into his Church
    to accept the cost and joy of discipleship
    to be his servants in the service of men,
    to proclaim the gospel to all the world
    and to resist the powers of evil,
    to share in Christ's baptism and eat at his table,
    to join him in his passion and victory.
He promises to all who trust him
    forgiveness of sins and fullness of grace,
    courage in the struggle for justice and peace,
    his presence in trial and rejoicing,
    and eternal life in his kingdom which has no end.

[2] The Anglican Articles, due to their relative brevity and primary concern with doctrine (though this latter is true of most of the other Confessions), contain little about Christian living. But it is interesting that, apart from the general assurance in Article XVII (*Of Predestination and Election*) and a negative view of works of supererogation (Article XIV) and of good works done before justification (Article XIII), norms for human existence are limited to three items: the permissibility of oaths in court (Article XXXIX), the duty of submission to civil authorities—no room for civil disobedience here! (Article XXXVII), and the error of socialism (Article XXXVIII).

[3] The injunctions included are on the whole sound—indeed edifying, displaying a good pastoral sense in filling out the aim of love of neighbor. As is true of the outlook during most centuries of Christian history, moral obligation is conceived of only in terms of one-to-one relationships, there being no hint of the responsibility of the Christian or of the Church to take positive action against patterns of society which block the fulfillment of persons. This is particularly noticeable in the Heidelberg Catechism (composed for the Church in the German Palatinate in 1563 and the primary document of the Reformed Church in Germany, the Netherlands, Hungary, and the United States) with its warm, humane presentation of duty to neighbor. The Anglican Catechism, a cut below the Heidelberg Catechism even in this regard, is marred further by a positive encouragement to be endorsive of existing social structures. Notice the holy water on the status quo: "To order myself lowly and reverently to all my betters:

None of the *liturgies* of the respective traditions, however, is lacking in affirmations and negations about what man is to be and do, and the motivations therefor. But they differ not only in the quantity of such material but also in emphases: by and large, the older liturgies say what they say in the framework of a pattern now which will insure heaven later while remaining silent with respect to implications relating to a sense of social responsibility which might motivate church members to seek to change the here and now. Newer forms have a more wholesome emphasis on life now and tend to present, with varying degrees of vividness, a call to social concern.

In the official statements, teaching and preaching of the various Churches, *consensus* is often used as a support for positions taken, but without attention to empirical data—only on a basis of assumption; yet it is obvious that consensus is lacking, on the most important realistic applications of ethical concern even within the Christian fold, let alone among men generally. Examples are almost too obvious and too numerous to mention: war (especially, at the present time, our policy *re* Vietnam), birth control, abortion, capital punishment, racial equality, the degree of socialization, for example, in extent of public medical benefits, mental health programs, public ownership), opportunity for the deprived (the "have-nots" in the decaying urban scene,[4] migratory farm workers[5]), attitudes toward homosexu-

---

... And to do my duty in that state of life unto which it shall please God to call me." (*Book of Common Prayer*, p. 580). In the presentation of this catechetical material elsewhere (in the same Prayer Book!) the first of these injunctions is softened to "And to order myself in that lowliness and reverence which becometh a servant of God," but the other injunction, reflecting the feudal and post-feudal class system is left undisturbed (Offices of Instruction, pp. 288–89).

[4] For example, the contention within various church regional bodies in various parts of the country with regard to involvement in community organization, particularly in collaboration with Dr. Saul Alinsky's Industrial Areas Foundation.

[5] For example: (1) in the struggle in Texas: cf. the active support of the workers by the Archbishop of San Antonio and by some of his priests with the disciplining by the same archbishop of two of his priests for publicly involving themselves in this issue as against the restraining policy

ality—both criminally and pastorally, use of alcohol,[6] sex,[7] and divorce and remarriage.[8] And in fact, as a number of recent studies show, it is in areas such as these that among the rank and file of the laity the official statements of the church bodies and the sermons of clergy are accorded the least authority.[9]

---

of the Bishop of Brownsville; (2) in the continuing struggle in California under the leadership of Cesar Chavez: cf. the official support given to the workers by the Roman Catholic Archdiocese of San Francisco and Los Angeles and the Episcopal Dioceses of California, with the resolution of the convention of the Episcopal Diocese of San Joaquin instituting a committee to investigate the actions and method of the farm workers organization.

[6] For example, the recent enactment by the Arkansas Legislature of a law prohibiting the giving of wine to persons under 21 in Holy Communion, with criminal sanctions up to 50 years in the penitentiary—an action taken under pressure from certain church leaders; and *per contra,* the immediate announcement by the Episcopal Bishop of Arkansas that he (and for this the priests of the diocese would also have his blessing) would defy the law—a position also taken forcefully by an official Lutheran spokesman. (The act has since been repealed.)

[7] For example, the recent controversy in Great Britain over the issuance of a non-absolutist report on the ethics of pre-marital sex by a committee of the British Council of Churches—simply an overt display of the increasingly open conflict between adherents of Code ethics and situation ethics in this regard. See two of the most recent books in this area: Joseph M. Fletcher, *Situation Ethics* (Philadelphia: Westminster Press, 1966), and the author's *You and the New Morality: 74 Cases.*

[8] Within the Roman Catholic Church, see Msgr. Victor J. Pospishil, *Divorce and Remarriage: Toward a New Catholic Teaching* (New York: Herder & Herder, 1967). For a summary of conflicting views and practices in the Episcopal Church, see the author's *A Time for Christian Candor* (New York: Harper & Row, 1964), Appendix A. Currently in the Church of England in connection with an official report (*Putting Asunder,* 1966) recommending more liberal divorce legislation by Parliament, although the Archbishop of Canterbury has stressed that the Church's bar to remarriage after divorce should be unchanged, there has come out in the open in debates in the Church Assembly widespread desire for reform in the *Church's* position.

[9] For example, Glock and Stark surveys cited in n. 36, p. 69, above. See the recent survey of American Roman Catholics in *Newsweek*, March 20, 1967, pp. 68 ff., which shows a wide variation of response to particular items of church teaching in such fields. Seven out of ten want the Church to lift the ban on contraception, but 59 per cent support the Church's stand on abortion (but only 40 per cent do in California, according to the Harris poll [See *Los Angeles Times,* May 21, 1966, p. 3]). However, while 55

In comparison with the silence, incompleteness, or indecisive-
ness of these five conventional religious authorities, the sixth
accepted source—*the Bible*—is a veritable gold mine of material
concerning man's behavior: codes of law, precepts on motivation and attitude, caveats, declarations as to cause and effect,
models and examples. No wonder that for generations it has
been thought to be the answer book par excellence for those
wanting to know what is right and what is wrong, because of
the sheer quantity of items, both generalizations and specifics
available in a concrete form.

Yet the reliability of the Scriptures for this purpose is highly
questionable for any who have approached it in either of the two
following ways: (1) reading it from cover to cover, which can
give only one impression of its ethical prescriptions: they are a
mishmash of idealism, common sense pragmatism, irrelevancy,
incomprehensibility, inspiration, superstition, sheer evil—and,
all through, flat contradiction; or (2) undertaking the more complex exercise of taking into account in connection with each
book—indeed each passage—the relevant cultural context, the
particular problem or issue to which each Biblical author was
addressing himself, the state of empirical knowledge at the
time, and the social conditioning and biases of the particular
writer—all of which can lead to little more than relativism. Few
people have ever done either; and until the era of modern Biblical
criticism, the second task was impossible of achievement.

It is hardly surprising, then, that throughout history Biblical
texts have been cited in support of mutually exclusive stances—

---

per cent would feel morally bound to follow their priest's judgment on
what books to read or avoid, only 21 per cent feel so bound with regard
to exhortations to integrate their neighborhood. Some 46 per cent would
not regard as sinful the refusal to receive Holy Communion from a Negro
priest. Quoted in Archbishop Robert E. Lucey of San Antonio: "To admit
that there are three persons in God and that Mary is a virgin mother caused
the Catholic no inconvenience. But when the pastor says to his people,
'You must love colored folks, you must treat Latin Americans as equals . . .
and, worst of all, you must not pay starvation wages to defenseless men
and women' too many Catholics declare that the pastor is taking things
too far."

both in personal morals and in social ethics, in support of both the status quo and of reform. That even the bibliolatrist Fundamentalists say that "the Devil [i.e., the other side] can quote Scripture" is a recognition of the fact that the Bible hardly offers a clear and unambiguous guide to life. That among purported Bible believers there is open conflict about "God's Law" shows that a high degree of selectivity goes on. And the fact of that process reveals that another standard is being used; the "proof texts" themselves are not the final thing. But to eliminate many of the contradictions and to justify rejection of a host of clear Biblical injunctions, many, relying on St. Paul, regard the law in the Old Testament as no longer applicable to the people of the New Israel. But one greater than Paul is reported to have said, "Think not that I have come to abolish the law. . . ," to have endorsed its every "iota and dot," and to have condemned "whoever relaxes one of the least of these commandments" (Matt. 5:17–19). In any case such scuttling of Old Testament laws is far from thoroughgoing: many people are absolutist about the Ten Commandments reported in Exodus and some still make dark reference to "the sin of Onan" (Gen. 38:8–10). They are not only not completely free of the Old Testament; they are not completely submissive to the New. To take just one example, it happens that in our day and time there is a fairly high correlation between those espousing literalism about the Bible (apparently they forget that the Bible includes the Sermon on the Mount, which is pacifistic to the point of impracticality) and those critical of the President's Vietnam policy on the ground that it is not achieving killing on wide enough a scale. (But one cannot say that they are not in line with Biblical ethics; illustrative of the selective process is the fact that here they are demonstrating loyalty to those Old Testament passages which endorse the killing of the enemies of God as meritorious—and that condemn failure to dispatch each and every one of them as deserving of God's wrath [1 Sam. 15].)

Apart from the Fundamentalists (in whose assertions logical snarls like the above are obvious), most people who take the

Bible seriously are endorsive of those texts which strike them as wholesome and good and ignore the rest. Though they are not usually aware of it, they are implying a norm of judgment—more often wisely than unwisely—which is apart from the Bible itself. Hence for them, though they do not recognize the fact—and would probably deny it if challenged, the Scriptures do not represent absolute authority.[10]

So the Bible—quantitatively the most promising of the six customary bases of authority with regard to moral decisions—joins the rest in inconsistency and relativity. This becomes apparent, in the case of each of these norms, by simply examining their content. Actually the same conclusion was compelled by the more basic exercise, in Chapter 4, of examining the sources of each. Therefore, if we are going to be able to make an affirmation about the style of life for man, we are required to start with facts, and then move to such affirmations by faith as plausibility may support.

There are two kinds of data available: what can be observed about persons as persons and what can be discerned about the intuitive response persons make to the displaying of a certain style of life in others—or in themselves.

One does not have to be an anthropologist or psychologist to recognize that persons are markedly different from the other creatures in the universe. Where does this difference lie?

It is generally assumed that each living person is cabined in by time and space, that his psyche can only function directly within the precise limits of his body. Effects which extend beyond his occupation of a limited space-time continuum are seen as the mechanical results of the space occupied by the body and the time at which the causative action occurs. As for the spanning of *space*, in giving a public address the speaker, as we say, gets his message "across" and to people he cannot touch even by the farthest stretching out of his arm. But the process does not involve any physical extension of himself beyond the borders of

[10] As to the nonfinality of the Bible as an authority for ethics see more fully the author's *You and the New Morality: 74 Cases*, Chaps. 2 and 3.

his own epidermis. Ears receive vibrations set up by the action of his tongue, mouth and larynx; eyes observe muscular changes in his face and movements of his arms and hands. Both the broadcasting and the reception are readily explainable by reliable laws of physics, physiology, and psychology; there is no necessity to aver that the speaker's psyche was directly extending itself beyond the space occupied by his physique. A similar analysis would apply to a telephone conversation between friends in San Francisco and London.

As for the spanning of *time*, a man on going to bed at 11:30 P.M. can ensure his awakening at precisely 7:30 A.M. by carefully setting his alarm clock before retiring. It is obvious that his psyche has not directly transcended the moment in which the causative action was taken, namely, half past eleven the night before. An engineering degree is not necessary in order to grasp the mechanics involved in this planned, deferred result. Much more complex to achieve, or even understand, is the programming of a timed series of operations of a rocket dispatched to the moon; but it is really of the same order as the setting of an alarm clock. The space technicians who have programmed future happenings have as individuals functioned within the spatial limits of their own bodies within the time span required to pre-set the controls. None of them is on his way to the moon or arrives there; and, if all goes according to plan, the various scheduled results would occur even if all of them were asleep or dead immediately or soon after the rocket takes off.

Implicit in the way all of this is said is a presupposition which prevails in our culture: that of a dualism of body and soul/mind/spirit. But with the progress of research and experience in the field of psychosomatic medicine, this dualism is becoming increasingly modified, verifying, to some degree on a scientific basis, interconnections between body and mind experienced throughout the ages and in some cases affirmed as religious truth (as in the case of the Christian Scientists). For example, psychosomatic study has revealed various causal connections between conscious attitudes, or patterns of the unconscious mind, and physical disorders. Now that it is perceived that there are many instances of the correlation of unresolved guilt feelings with malfunction of limbs, such healing as that attributed to Jesus in Matthew 9: 1–7 ("Take heart, my son; your sins are forgiven . . . Rise, take up your bed and go home"), while not supplied with additional historical verification, nevertheless moves out of the realm of "miracle" into the arena of "the natural."

The first phase of progress in psychosomatic medicine was the verification of such connections between psychic conditions and physical disorders, the former being perceived as causative of the latter. More recently, attention is being focused on an apparent reverse causality (one can call this "somatopsychic" medicine): biochemical sources of emotional and mental disorders. It has been found, for example, that there occurs an as yet unsatisfactorily explained corruption of natural adrenalin into adrenalutin, which appears to have effects very similar to the psychedelic synthetic, mescaline. Both substances place an individual in a schizophrenic state. An antidote (massive doses of a common vitamin) has been discovered which restores the schizophrenic to a normal state of mind in many cases. Thus, encouraged researchers are seeking to broaden the base of a somatic solution to what had recently been conceived of as a psychiatric problem. But apparently chemistry is not all that is involved. Experience so far has shown that the neutralizing of the deleterious substance (by the intake of the chemical antidote) does not of itself achieve stability.

Here there is a parallel in experience with alcoholism. To stop drinking may leave the victim "dry" but does not necessarily make him "sober": hence the recovered alcoholic's involvement in A.A. has a therapeutic as well as a preventive role. Likewise, the counteracting of the systemic effects of adrenaluten is not enough: experience is showing that achievement of stability requires therapy (for example, participation in the recently formed Schizophrenics Anonymous or individual psychiatric counseling). The obvious reason for this would seem to be that the period of chemically caused psychological distortion has left effects in the psychological makeup. But it is also highly probable that psychosomatic (as contrasted with somatopsychic) causation has been simultaneously involved all along. To take our example, the conditioning of the unconscious and/or conscious mind may provide part of the explanation why the adrenalin normally present in everyone corrupts into adrenaluten in the bodies of some people.

The same consideration applies in the case of alcohol. A.A. counselors are pragmatically quite right in their urgent insistence that the first thing is immediately and permanently to stop the intake rather than to ponder what may be the psychological or situational sources of the alcoholic's temptation to imbibe. Nevertheless, psychological factors have been operative and are often discernible, either by psychiatric help or self-reflection on the part of the alcoholic once dry, which distinguish the effects that alcohol—even in approximately the same quantities on given occasions—has on alcoholics and on nonalcoholics: hence the quite separately recognized category of "the heavy drinker."[11]

It would be easy from data of this sort to conclude that what we have thought of as man's "spirit" is coextensive to the point of identity with his body. Indeed some go so far as to maintain, as does Professor Corliss Lamont, that the findings of the sciences that deal with man "have inexorably led to the proposition that mind or personality is a function of the body."[12] It is true that increasing research displays a greater degree of interconnection between what we customarily speak of as soul and body (whether properly conceived of on a causal basis or on one or another acausal base). Certainly no longer viable is the Cartesian view of man tellingly referred to as "the ghost in the machine." But also evident is the fact that man is more than his body. Simultaneously with our awareness of another person's

---

[11] See Marty Mann, *New Primer on Alcoholism* (New York: Rinehart, 1958), Chap. 4.

[12] *The Illusion of Immortality* (New York: Philosophical Library, 1963), p. 113.

physical reality is awareness of *more*, a transcendence, a "beyond within."

This *more* is displayed in two ways. First, man transcends himself, his immediate context, and his larger environment. Entailed in this plainly observable fact is an "over-and-aboveness." Only man has the capacity of recognizing a world over against him. "An animal's 'image of the world,'" Dr. Martin Buber has pointed out, "is nothing more than the dynamic presences bound up with one another with bodily memory to the extent required by the functions of life which are to be carried out. This image depends on, it clings to the animal's activities. It is only man who replaces this unsteady conglomeration . . . by a unity which can be thought by him as existing for itself."[13] He illustrates this:

An animal's actions are concerned with the future and the future of its young, but only man imagines the future: the beaver's dam is extended in a time-realm but the planted tree is rooted in a world of time and he who plants the first tree is he who will expect the Messiah.[14]

And this is true in relation to himself. He can look at himself (as it were, one self looking at another) and decide that he does not like the way that he is; and thus he can achieve loss or gaining of weight, reordering of priorities, reselection of values.

Second, the *more* in a man is directly apprehended by another of the same species who knows him as a person. A man can know another man as body. His physician can inspect him, weigh and measure him, just as an object can be surveyed. But the physician, as well as others who have no special preoccupation with one or more aspects of the man's physical frame, can know the unique and unifying, transcending "center" which makes him a *thou*, not just an *it*. There are almost limitless depths to what can be perceived: the more opportunities for re-

13 *The Knowledge of Man*, selected essays, edited, with introductory essay by Maurice Friedman (New York: Harper & Row, 1965), p. 62. See a discerning review by Rabbi S. E. Karff in *Journal of Religion*, Vol. XLVII, No. 1, pp. 52–53.

14 *Ibid*. The last phrase touchingly reflects what is a high priority in Israel; as for the eschatological motif, see pp. 46–47, above, and pp. 196–197, below.

lationship, the more time open for knowing, and the greater the intensity of focus on a person, the more is realized of that which is already real and the more is appreciated "the beyond in the midst."

In every such knowing an utterly unique center of reality is perceived; to the degree that the uniqueness is not recognized, to that degree the knowing has been superficial. But through the multitudes of such particular apprehensions of persons there is inevitably incurred a generic: the transcendence of man. This transcendence is shown in a goodly number of ways—among them man's capacity to tie together past, present, and future. He remembers and can reflect upon the content of his memories endorsively or critically, and can thus learn from the past. He can plan for the future, make commitments about it, and fulfill them. And all at once both his past and future are a genuine part of his present. He is not only creature of environment; he and his fellows can be creators of environment. He not only has been evolved; he is an evolver of what shall be. He not only can observe particular things, he can derive generic categories and, beyond that, he can reach (soundly or unsoundly) abstract notions of vast proportions. He can articulate to other persons his particular impressions, his generic categories, and his over-all abstractions. He can, in good measure at least, reveal himself to another or to others; and he can conceive the revelation of another self.

In short, a thing is properly *referred to* as "it"; a man can be *addressed* as "you." All that this distinction implies is a matter of empirical observation. And equally observable is the fact that persons differ from one another. Also the range of difference, in each distinguishable aspect, is enormous; in this important regard what has been increasingly noticed since the Renaissance (and, incidentally, has been made more the case by the very fact of the noticing) has been confirmed, in more recent times, by multiphasic psychological testing.

It does not require a great leap of faith, then, to proceed to affirm two things. Persons are more valuable than things. Each person is uniquely valuable. Not entailed in these propositions but closely connected is another: a person should not be treated as a thing.

Persons are treated as things in two ways, one quite obvious, one somewhat less obvious. Very perceptive is an idiom frequently heard. The verb in, for example, "He just *used* her" carries with it the assessment that he valued someone no more highly than he would value a thing—just as a means to some end of his.

Recognition of valuation of persons is lacking also when their uniqueness is ignored. Discrimination, in many circles, has become a "bad word" in our society. But actually it can mean a good thing, a positive recognition of human uniqueness. An instructor who displays responsibility in constructing a soundly evaluative and carefully balanced set of examination questions and exercises similar responsibility is a discerning grading of the papers is witnessing to one of the most wonderful aspects of reality— the marked difference between, and utter uniqueness of, individual persons. A personnel director does this in his work of screening applicants for employment and his channeling of the successful ones into various departments of the firm's activities. And this happens too in many less organized decisions, like choosing dinner guests or bridge partners. But in all such activities, and in many others, discrimination in another sense of the word has been a characteristic of group and individual behavior. Decisions are made about persons and about their status, the scope of their opportunities for development and rewards, their pleasures, their chance to love and be loved, and all aspects of their environment—all this not on a basis of personal and individual differences in quality, merit, or charm, but on a group basis. Employed is some category: race, ethnic background, religious affiliation or lack of it, sex, age, social class, wealth, etc. The objects of such decisions are persons, but persons denied (by the very fact of the use of such categories) an essential aspect of personhood: uniqueness. Thus, *ipso facto,* persons have been reified, "thingified."

Any home owner with even minimum expectancies for an environment of quiet, safety, and attractiveness would feel threatened at the prospect of the moving in next door to him of a family—black or white—whose known past performance in other localities gives reason to believe that their house will go unpainted and unrepaired, that their lawn will become overgrown, that trash will accumulate around the front door, that their children and their accustomed companions will wreck his shrubbery and pilfer the tools in his garage, and that their customary home social life is less frequently quiet dialogue before a fireplace than a drunken brawl. For him to plead with the owner about to move not to sell to this particular prospect is discrimination—and discrimination which is both justified and responsible. But, on the unverified assumption that more than likely a Negro family will act out all or most of the above mentioned unpleasantries, to take steps personally—or, as is all too common, corporately—to keep the neighborhood "all white" is to view persons as things, and treat them as such. Even more elaborate a system of depersonalization is the highly organized —and highly successful—program, virtually national in scope, of realty boards to maintain ghettoization of communities.

There are many people who would see racial discrimination in housing as wrong (or at least who might not vote No on a resolution about it in a church convention) who are prepared to justify rules barring Negroes (or even Jews) from social clubs. Commonplace is "A man is entitled to choose his social companions." Actually, that is a sound statement—and there is no accounting for tastes. But a club regulation barring people of specified categories is not an implementation of freedom of choice: it is a restriction of it. It forecloses even the possibility of choosing a particular minority-group person, say a Negro or a Jew, who would make an excellent and rewarding social companion. True acknowledgment of a speciality of personhood means this: personal discrimination, Yes; group discrimination (reification), No.

All of this points to the validity of Martin Buber's distinction between *I–Thou* and *I–it*, and to the priority of the first quality of relationship over the second. And this, *both* in the Divine-human context and in the interpersonal context. This significant insight, of utmost importance in itself, is also a nexus between the conclusion we have drawn on a basis of the easily observable distinction between persons and things *and* an equally important conclusion we can draw from characteristic recurrent instances of internal reaction in persons when they witness or reflect upon vivid instances or consistent patterns of life that display high valuation of the I–thou level of relationship.

This nexus established, we move to this second category of data. What we have been talking about up to this point is what a person, as contrasted with a thing, is and the *ought* which plausibly arises from the *is*. We should now take note of what is a common response in individuals when they see, hear about, or read of consistent acting out of this *ought*. Important to an empirical foundation for a faith-affirmation of an all-embracing model for human fulfillment are the data about human transcendence and the conclusions we have inferred from it. But equally important to this same larger end is another body of significant data—experience and reports about what happens inside persons in reaction to real-life situations in which are exhibited a man's living out what these conclusions imply.

A mother in a rapidly burning house, herself already seriously burned, calls out to a passer-by for immediate help in extricating her child from under a fallen ceiling beam. Just before noticing her he saw that the entire roof was near collapse; yet he rushes in and works steadily with the mother until the child is released, all three reaching the street just as the entire structure collapses. Up to this point the narration simply serves to illustrate, by way of an externally observable event, the importance of persons and their treatment. But this is not the end of the story. Three other people arrive on the scene just as the stranger, now badly burned too, emerges from the collapsing house with the child in his arms followed by the mother. The observers easily learn what happened. From that very moment of awareness it is most likely that

in each will have arisen, instantaneously and intuitively, a clearly
discernible feeling about the rescuer, one with at least three
facets:

    a. Sheer admiration for the rescuer of the child;

    b. A "good feeling" that there are human beings capable of
       acting as this particular one did; and

    c. For each in introspection (depending upon his past per-
       formance and on his current self-assessment), one or more
       of such feelings as guilt, hope that he might be courageous
       and loving enough similarly to respond spontaneously to
       as grave a challenge, fear that he might not—in other
       words, wanting to be, to have been and/or to become
       that way.

In short, the intuitive response in these newcomers to the scene
would probably be a mixture of admiration, joy, and aspiration.
Now this very response is a *fact*. It would be one clearly recog-
nizable as such by each particular person so responding.

No other direct evidence of the reaction is possible. Should he
blurt it out promptly to someone, there is a high likelihood of its
reality, as is recognized by an interesting rule of evidence in the
Anglo-Saxon common law (which is based not on legislation
but on various foci of centuries of corporate human experience).
As is generally known, hearsay evidence is not admissible in
court because from this breadth of experience has developed a
generic suspicion grounded in fallibility of memory and the possibility of contrivance. But among the long-recognized exceptions
to the prohibition of hearsay is one called *res gestae*: what a person utters, without time for reflection, at a dramatic moment, is
admissible in evidence. Granted that such is not absolute proof;
but the likelihood of the statement's not being true to the facts
has been reduced to a minimum by the special context. So here.
But can we take seriously reports of such inner experiences—
and of inner experiences of other types which are as definitely
real to the person recounting them—which are commonly articulated to others well after the event which occasioned them? On
any one such account we would not want to build much. But it

is obvious that in the area we are talking about such a report does not stand alone.

To return to the example: One of the observers tells a friend he meets a half hour later about the rescue and the rescuer. It would be unlikely indeed that the friend would fail to respond—though perhaps less vividly because he was not personally present. Assume that there was good press coverage. Thousands of people have brought before them the same vignette. Many, far from the scene and with no personal involvement in the occasion, will have a similar inner response to the objective event—though perhaps one more quickly forgotten.

Even more widespread and recurring generation after generation is the response to notable instances in history of the display in particular honored figures of a style of life which can be summed up in some such combination of words as *truth-courage-love*.[15] Primary for many Christians is the servant image which emerges from the narratives about Jesus in the New Testament (in contrast to the more obviously Essene-influenced picturization of Him as the powerful guarantor of victory for the Elect by imminent intervention from Heaven[16]); but volumes of history, biographies, and "lives of the Saints" from varied religious traditions are replete with illustrations. To mention a few: Buddha, whose Enlightenment had almost brought him to Nirvana, turns back, as it were, that he may assist others along the same path.[17] Socrates, his life at stake, wavers not a moment from his loyalty

[15] See the author's *You and the New Morality: 74 Cases*, Chap. 7, especially p. 56.

[16] Since the author's *What Is This Treasure* is devoted primarily to Christology, analysis of the estimate of Jesus and his uniqueness by faith-affirmation is not undertaken again in the present work. To use phraseology familiar in one of the author's professions, this important and complex topic is "hereby filed by title and incorporated herein as if fully set forth." See also the illuminating analyses in John Knox, *The Humanity and the Divinity of Christ* (New York: Cambridge University Press, 1967); S. G. F. Brandon, *Jesus and the Zealots* (Manchester University Press, 1967); and Joe Edward Barnhart, "Incarnation and Process Philosophy," *Religious Studies*, Vol. 2, No. 2 (1967), pp. 225–32.

[17] Regarding the first three illustrations, see more fully the author's *What Is This Treasure*, Chap. 2.

to truth at all costs and to "the only wise God,"[18] trusts that that to which he had been witnessing would survive his execution, affirms love of his accusers and judges, and thereafter—in prison, awaiting the end—displays serenity and confidence in what lies ahead beyond the grave. The unnamed righteous man, the object of hatred and resentment in the Wisdom of Solomon, Chapter 2, steadfastly, with abiding confidence in God, manifests a consistent stance, independently different from other men— hence provoking bitter and insistent resentment, faced the certain consequence of "shameful death" (v. 20), but still would not cease from speaking the truth as he saw it.

Such persons come in all shapes and sizes, live and act in all times and places, and are embraced within various religions— and none. A unique combination of these variants provides the context of what one intuitively responds to in learning about Samuel Joseph Isaac Schereschewsky, a Jewish Episcopal missionary bishop who served in China and first translated the Scriptures from Hebrew and Greek into Mandarin and Easy Wenli.[19]

A rabbinical student in Russian Lithuania, Schereschewsky came across a Hebrew translation of the New Testament and was set to thinking about the possibility that Jesus really was the Messiah of his people. His spiritual quest led him to Germany for study and subsequently to New York City, where he eventually prepared for the priesthood of the Episcopal Church at the General Theological Seminary. His brilliance was such that there it was intimated to him that he might look forward to joining the faculty; but at this time he was very much influenced by one of the first missionaries to China, Bishop Boone, and he decided to join him and use his linguistic abilities to translate the Scriptures into Chinese. He set sail, learning the Chinese language during the voyage (which, of course, took longer in those days).

[18] Cf. 1 Tim. 1:17.
[19] The account which follows is adapted from the author's *Beyond Anxiety*, pp. 60–62. See more fully James Muller, *Apostle of China* (New York: Morehouse, 1937).

Since Schereschewsky felt strongly that the most important thing to be done in the missionary enterprise was the translation of the Scriptures into the native tongue, when he was elected Bishop of the missionary area by the American House of Bishops, he declined. However, when he was elected again he reluctantly accepted—though he afterwards sought to withdraw his acceptance and five years later express the hope that the Church would permit him to resign and resume his work of translation. Then one day he suffered a sunstroke and became almost totally paralyzed—save for the middle finger on the right hand. Forced to return to America, he immediately set to work to complete his work of translation. Since no Chinese scholar was available to serve as scribe and he was unable to write himself, Schereschewsky poked out on a typewriter with his one finger the English equivalents of the Chinese characters; and so eager was he to push on with the work that when his one active finger would grow tired he would stamp out the letters with a small stick clutched in his fist. He produced two translations, one in Easy Wenli for the common man, and one in Mandarin for the educated. He set sail with his manuscript to China, where, with the aid of Chinese assistants, he published the manuscript and then proceeded to prepare reference Bibles in each of the dialects.

One week after he brought this work to a close he died—a fulfillment of his prayer: "I am never without pain . . . when I have done this book I pray the dear Lord to take me to Himself." Schereschewsky thus provided tools which set forward the whole missionary effort—of course, quite beyond the limits of his own Church—much more than his own individual leadership in the mission field could have done. And he was grateful that he had been enabled, because of his paralysis, to complete the really important thing. He was able to say: "I have sat in this chair for over twenty years. It seemed very hard at first. But God . . . kept me for the work for which I am best fitted."

Radically different in background, role, and mode of articulation was Mohandas Karamchand Gandhi.[20] His life and achieve-

20 *Autobiography*, English translation, limited edition (London, 1948).

ment as the founder of free India need not be retold here, and well known, too, is the fact that he has been the inspiration of the philosophy of nonviolence which has been such a significant component in the witness in this country—by Christians, Jews, and secularists alike—against racial injustice. Perhaps less well known is the breadth of influences which helped to form him: for example, John Ruskin, Leo Tolstoy, the Indian poet Raychandbhai, the New Testament, and the Bhagavad-Gita of his own Hindu background. Equally important in our perception of what there is about him and in him that has evoked such an effective response in persons of widely diverse types and cultures is how he viewed matters in the midst of great suffering and what for other men would be frustration and occasion for bitterness and hatred. So we are fortunate that we can read such words of his as these:

> Let our first act every morning be the following resolve: I shall not fear anyone on earth. I shall fear only God. I shall not bear ill-will towards anyone. I shall not submit to injustice from anyone. I shall conquer untruth by truth and in resisting untruth I shall put up with all suffering.
> *Ahimsa* [nonviolence] is not merely a negative state of harmlessness, but it is a positive state of love, of doing good even to the evildoer . . . the active state of *ahimsa* requires you to resist the wrongdoer by dissociating yourself from him even though it may offend him or injure him physically.[21]

So significant in the lives of the people of two races, David Livingstone [22] is probably the only man in history whose remains have been buried in two continents—literally, his heart in Africa and the rest of his body in England. Sent as a medical missionary to South Africa, from the beginning he was compelled by a desire to push further out to bring the Gospel and healing to remote places, learning the languages and the ways of life as he went.

[21] Mohandas Karamchand Gandhi, *The Story of My Experiments with Truth* (Ahmedabad: Navajivan Press, 1927–29). Translated from the original in Gujarati by Mahadev Desai.
[22] H. M. Stanley, *How I Found Livingstone* (New York: Scribner Amity & Co., 1872).

He faced the opposition of the Boers and also the conservatism of his supporting Missionary Society—particularly when, having been shocked by the horrors of the slave trade, he felt that exploration was primary in order to learn more about economically feasible trade routes from the interior to undercut the apparent need of slavery. His vast and horrendously dangerous journeys, which separated him from wife and family, also brought him repeated periods of serious illness. (And when he was able to arrange for his wife to join him she died of fever.)

The result of his efforts and writing about what he saw and experienced not only was the catalyst for bringing to Africa an army of explorers and missionaries but also in arousing in people all over the world a feeling against slave trading. Throughout all the strain, frustration and physical suffering he displayed such a gentlemanly and loving spirit that he was not only loved and admired—even by the Arab slave traders whom he opposed—but, in spite of his own modesty, was treated as a form of superior being. To any who read the story there are any number of particular episodes which vividly manifest truth-courage-love. One will suffice here.

In November, 1853, he made his difficult journey from Sesheki on the Zambesi River through unknown country to the West Coast of Africa with a score or so of Africans in the hope of establishing an adequate trade route. During the six months he had no fewer than twenty-seven bouts of fever and was in constant danger from hostile tribes. Arriving at Loananda, broken in health but buoyed by the success of the expedition, he was at once invited by several ship captains to take passage back home to England—a prospect which offered reunion with his family, recovery of health, and great honors. But though strongly urged, he felt his acceptance of any of these offers to be out of the queston because he was sure the Africans could not get back home by themselves. It was clear to him that he must return with them—a return which was even more perilous—burdened by the disappointment that neither of the routes, going or coming, would fulfill his larger purpose of finding a trade route. Undaunted, Livingstone continued to try to fulfill this aim, in the process exploring a third of Africa and providing mapping which has served as definitive well into the twentieth century. Up to the very end he pursued this task to within a few days of his death. At the beginning of the last December of his life he began an expedition to the west in the direction of Lake Mweru. The rain poured pitilessly down and food became scarce. Weakened by loss of blood and the pain of acute dysentery with him, he refused to be carried. One night he became separated from his party and spent the night on a hill near the tiny village of what is now Malawi. In the morning when his followers found him he was in a much worsened condition, but still continued to march. At last, however, they were forced to make a camp by the side of a river. As night fell the watchmen lighted their fires and sat silent and dejected. Livingstone lay on a bed of sticks and grass, by him a box with a candle. When his boy looked in to see if everything was in order he found Livingstone beside the bed on his knees, praying. And it was in this way that David Livingstone's spirit quietly departed and left his tired, pain-racked body at last at rest.

The sorrowing natives carefully cut his heart out and buried it beneath a great tree, for they said, "His heart was for Africa." His body they dried and carried on a journey as full of peril as any ever undertaken by Livingstone himself, halfway across Africa to the hands of the British in Zanzibar.

He actually never found the trade route which he sought for years with the most astonishing perseverance of a brilliant mind and a sick body—well aware that he had long been rejected by the London Missionary Society for his having given primacy to this task. But the glory of his courageous striving and the infectious quality of his unswerving purpose acted out in love is regarded as the mortal blow to the slave trade.

"Is it heresy," the official weekly of the Roman Catholic Diocese of Worcester (Mass.) asked, "to think that a Unitarian Universalist minister is a Saint of the Church, and to wish that

and pray that deep in our hearts the American hierarchy in a
true ecumenical spirit would recognize him as such and petition
the Holy See for his canonization? We think not."[23] This was
a "first" and a vivid example of what has been discussed above
as the spontaneous intuitive response to episodes which display
truth-courage-love. The minister was the Rev. James Reeb,
whose bludgeoning to death in downtown Selma, Alabama, on
March 9, 1965, more than any single thing galvanized the conscience of the nation and promptly evoked the President's Voting
Rights Bill.

"America needed a model, an example of Christian love such
as it had not had before," the diocesan paper continued. ". . .
[n]ow we have him in James Reeb. He was what we would hope
to be: true witness to Christ in the marketplace. . . . He lost his
life; but he won that for which we have all come to earth."

A particularly touching example of the type of response we
have been talking about was furnished by a letter Mrs. Reeb
received two days after Jim's death. A medal was enclosed with
it and the letter read:

Dear Mrs. Reeb:
  Twenty years ago I was awarded the enclosed medal. The citation
read in part—"volunteered to accompany a platoon of light tanks in
order to point out targets for their effective fire—he advanced
through the street of town in advance of the armored vehicles—
firing his sub-machine gun at targets of opportunity."
  Your late husband, Reverend Reeb, volunteered to accompany his
fellowmen against a force of greater threat to the principles of our
country, than my opponent, the German soldier.
  Reverend Reeb was unarmed except for his convictions; his "armed
support" was the songs and prayers of the oppressed.
  Would you please give this medal to your oldest son, John—his
father was a much barver American than I.
                                        Sincerely,
                                            JOHN D. McCARTHY[24]

---

[23] The Rev. Duncan Howlett, D.D., *No Greater Love* (New York: Harper
& Row, 1966), p. 226.
[24] *Ibid.*, pp. 233–34.

This illustration does not require reflection on the past; it is part of the present. For the author and many of his readers it is "closer to home." For example, down at Selma at the same time were the author and one who has served as pastor to both the author and the deceased.[25]

Violent death is always tragic, whatever the context, and when it occurs in the pursuit of a good cause it speaks for itself. But such an instance serves more fully as a mirror of meaning and effect on others when it has been the climax of what can be discerned as a consistent style of life.

Jim was raised a fundamentalist in the Presbyterian Church. Throughout his youth and college days his way of life and witness showed unremitting loyalty to his convictions. During clinical training courses at the New Jersey Neuro-Psychiatric Institute and field work at the Philadelphia General Hospital, what he was learning and experiencing was challenging much of his authority-based theology. He was coming more and more to the conviction that he should not take a church after graduation from Princeton Theological Seminary but should seek a chaplaincy post instead. He was appointed chaplain at the Hospital. From almost the beginning of his field work he sensed that the realities perceived in dealing with the broken bodies and minds of living men and women did not match the theology by which Christianity was explained and defended in seminary lectures; and he resisted the common temptation to keep in separate compartments his theology and his experience as interpreted by psychiatric knowledge.

The inner struggle intensified but he externalized it by seeking counsel from older clergy, receiving a variety of answers, any one of which, for a different kind of man, could have served as a basis for rationalization. He decided that he should become a Unitarian. The opposition of his counselors was apparent and vigorous were his parents' attempts to dissuade him. His con-

25 The Rev. Harry Scholefield, D.D., Minister of the First Unitarian Church of San Francisco, who was at the First Unitarian Church of Philadelphia at a turning point in Jim Reeb's life.

sistent recognition of the place of psychological factors in personal decision-making led him to a psychiatrist to check out his motives. Jim was well aware that unconscious motives which were changing his religion might be much more powerful than those with which he was struggling consciously, but after four sessions the psychiatrist concluded the movement of thought was due to two deep-lying characteristics which had been in Jim since his boyhood. As Dr. Howlett reports it:

The first was his passion for intellectual consistency—his desire to establish a principle and then to line everything else up in accordance with it. The same demand that once made him accept everything in the Bible as literally true now required him to believe literally whatever his church professed. Again it was all or nothing.

A second and closely related factor was Jim's honesty. Honesty was so deeply ingrained in his nature that he could only use words to mean what they actually said. Why this was true was a complex matter. But that it was true no one could doubt. Jim understood very well the need to ascertain and state the true meaning of ancient words written in another language and in a very different cultural context. But he strongly objected to giving ancient words meanings they never had at all in order to make them useful in the modern age. He found the practice, so widespread in contemporary religion, no less objectionable when applied to the Westminster Confession than when used on Bible texts.

Why give so much effort to stretching old language into modern meanings? he asked. Why not let the Bible and the creeds say what they said for their own purposes and in their own time? Then, in new words designed for the purpose, let men set forth new religious concepts as they emerged in their minds. To him things had to feel right to be right. And it didn't feel right to him when, for pious purposes, words which patently meant one thing were made to mean something else. Since it did not feel right he could not bring himself to do it.[26]

Considerable delay followed between his first step and his being received in the Unitarian ministry; but his sense of integrity required him to resign his chaplaincy. He found a post as a Y.M.C.A. youth director and served for two years, an inter-

26 *Op. cit.*, p. 88.

lude that played an important part in the ultimate outcome, for, added to his experience of individual distress and grief, came what was direct and sustained confrontation with the deprivations and stresses created for Negroes by patterns of racial discrimination. In 1959 he began a happy and effective ministry as Dr. Howlett's assistant at All Souls' Church in Washington, D. C. That going to Selma and what happened to him there was not an isolated event, the meaning of which would have to be inferred, is shown by his increasing involvement in Washington in work for the deprived, for example, through the University Neighborhoods Council, and by what he was saying in sermons.

"We shall find no security in existence," Jim had said in one of his first Washington sermons, "if the mere continuing of our life is our final goal. A man never has been willing and never shall be content merely to live." Then he asked, "Is there nothing worth risking the end of one's life for? Are there no dreams or goals so important that we can risk our own destruction to gain them?" [27] This was consistent with a student sermon preached more than a decade before: "A Christian willingly chooses to sacrifice himself that other men might be saved. Wherever right is struggling with wrong he takes his place on the battleline. Wherever men are in misery or sickness he gives of himself to relieve their suffering."[28] But he was strongly committed to the philosophy of nonviolence. This he spelled out in his closing sermon after five years at All Souls. He recognized that "there is in each of us [Negro or white] this temptation to be violent," but he saw that if change is rightly to come "we are going to have to really take upon ourselves a continuing and disciplined effort with no real hope that in our lifetime we are going to be able to take a vacation from the struggle for justice."[29]

At this last service he used as the pastoral prayer one written

[27] *Ibid.*, p. 233.
[28] *Ibid.*, p. 178.
[29] *Ibid.*

two thousand years ago by the Roman Stoic and logician, Eusebius:

> May I be no man's enemy, and may I be the friend of that which is eternal and abides. . . . May I never devise evil against any man; if any devise evil against me, may I escape . . . without the need of hurting him. May I love, seek and attain only that which is good. May I wish for all men's happiness and envy none. . . . When I have done or said what is wrong, may I never wait for the rebuke of others, but always rebuke myself until I make amends. . . . May I win no victory that harms either me or my opponent. . . . May I reconcile friends who are wroth with one another. May I, to the extent of my power, give all needful help . . . to all who are in want. May I never fail a friend in danger. . . . May I respect myself. . . . May I always keep tame that which rages within me. . . . May I never discuss who is wicked and what wicked things he has done, but know good men and follow in their footsteps.[30]

His concluding prayer was brief: "Let all who live in freedom, won by sacrifice of others, be untiring in the task begun, till every man on earth is free."[31]

When Martin Luther King issued the call for clergy to go to Selma, Jim quickly made his decision. When he told Marie, his wife, her lower lip began to tremble. In her mind, as in the minds of millions of Americans, was what she had seen on the television screen not twenty-four hours before—the horror of the bull-whippings and face-stompings in Selma on that unforgettable Sunday night. She thought of their four children and of their life together. "I don't want you to go," was her response. "There are others to go. You belong here."

"No," he replied, "I belong there."

"All right," she said, "I know . . ."[32]

She did know. Step after step in his short life had said it. Right now they were living in the slums of Boston so that he could be actually a part of the lives of those he was now serving under the auspices of the American Friends Service Committee.

[30] As edited by Jerome Nathanson, *Look*, March 22, 1955.
[31] Howlett, *op. cit.*, p. 178.
[32] *Ibid.*, p. 197.

He had loved All Souls' and the comfortable life in Washington; but his part-time community involvement there was not enough. Taking a substantial cut in salary (he'd had to borrow money for his trip to Selma), he found a post which would allow him to be entirely "along side" of the deprived: all-embracingly and literally a *ministry of presence*.

In life and in death he displayed the meaning of a familiar passage: Let this mind be in you which was *also* in Jesus, who being in the image of God, emptied himself, did not care about reputation, took the role of a servant, and was obedient even to death.[33]

He, of whom these words are so descriptive, is the one whose deposition decree from the Presbyterian Church included the adjective "heretical" and whom the Roman Catholic diocesan editors in proposing canonization called "saint." Both were correct. He was *heretical* in the two senses of the word we have identified in Chapter I, the popular and the etymological: his views did not square with the confession of faith of a particular denomination, and he "chose for himself" what seemed true and real.[34] And he was a *saint* in two senses: in the popular sense —good; in the etymological sense—holy; that is, dedicated, committed. (His life was a yes-saying to the questions he himself had set: "Is there nothing worth risking the end of one's life for? Are there no dreams or goals so important . . . ?")

Yet there was, we can be sure, an ecumenical bridge in the *response:* after his death, the reaction was doubtless no less vivid among the members of the Presbytery court which had uttered the word "heretical" than it was in the Roman Catholic editors who uttered the word "saint."

The examples chosen from a span of two and a half millennia include a pagan philosopher, a Hindu religious revolutionary,[35]

---

[33] Selected and adapted from Phil. 2:5–8.

[34] Cf. pp. 2–3 and p. 14, above.

[35] Buddha was a Hindu, not a Buddhist, just as Jesus—contrary to popular impression—was a Jew, not a Christian.

a Jewish construct or "type," a Hindu political revolutionary, a Jewish Episcopal bishop, an evangelical Anglican explorer, and a Unitarian "worker-priest."[36] Just as we have seen in the case of specific instances of religious (or peak) experience,[37] there is a generic character to the truth-courage-love style of life and to the response of others to it, regardless of the conflicting theologies which it may be used to help prove.

Each instance of human response to each such example responded to is a *fact*. It is a fact not verifiable in a laboratory nor directly by witnesses other than the given respondent. But the instances of response run to the millions and billions and there is a generic character to them, just as the instances of that to which there is such response are countless—in all times and places. Too, the instances which are responded to share a common ground; that which we saw as legitimately inferable from observation and comparison of persons and of things, namely, that persons are not to be treated as things and that the uniqueness of each separate person is to be regarded as precious.

So under our method, as already analyzed,[38] it is plausible for one to infer from all these data that the best style of life is that so well characterized by Dietrich Bonhoeffer (who himself could appropriately have been included in the illustrations given) in his phrase pointing primarily to the servant-image of Jesus: the man for others.

If the personal transcendence which this affirmation honors is so important in the here and now, it is natural next to ask whether it abides or whether death after a few short years brings an end to it.

[36] When Jim Reeb was being interviewed as a Presbyterian for the Y job, and as a Unitarian for the South Boston job, in each case he denied that he was "leaving the ministry."

[37] See pp. 131–36, above.

[38] See pp. 75–81, above.

CHAPTER VII

LIFE AFTER DEATH

One of the first major beliefs to go for most people when they jettison a conventional authority-based scheme of doctrine is the conviction about life after death. The rejection is commonplace, regardless of how the matter has been viewed or phrased in the religious tradition or semantics of the person: whether as the resurrection of the body, as eternal life, or as immortality. Even among the more orthodox who would not make an outright denial of this doctrine, there is, as statistics show,[1] a fairly high degree of doubt about survival after death.

Often this doubt is masked by emphasis on other motifs when a situation arises which requires talking about it. One whole profession (and one not the least insensitive to public relations and personal psychology—in fact there are courses in these fields in their professional schools), that of mortuary science, has over the years developed a terminology which apparently mirrors—and in turn helps form—a widespread "grass roots" doctrine among lay people and even among some clergy. Its verbal cornerstones are the two R's of REMEMBRANCE and REST.

The deceased individual is believed to live on in the accomp-

[1] Glock and Stark, *Religion and Society in Tension* (Chicago: Rand McNally & Co., 1965), p. 98.

lishments of his earthly days and in the memory of those who
were aware of these accomplishments or who at least knew him.
Especially is this expected to be true of those closest to him
(who, incidentally, have an opportunity to express their ap-
preciation of his life in varying degrees—sometimes gauged by
the expense of the coffin and of the burial plot). Death is not
to be mentioned: he has "passed," "passed away" (for the more
tacitly pessimistic), or "passed on." The thought is really never
finished: passed (on or away) to what?

This is implicitly answered by the companion R: he is at
rest (for either the more literal devotees of the doctrine or the
unthinking, this conviction can be visibly expressed in varying
degrees by the quality of the padding—or even of the rubber-
foam mattress—provided for the remains.) As a summary of
these tenets of doctrine, an old reassuring word (in good standing in a particular period of Greek philosophy, with a slender
base in some Biblical books and a somewhat wider base in some
Christian writings and homiletics), *immortality*—in a most
minimal sense—is frequently employed. Most of the bereavement notes and face-to-face consoling words expressed—even
by church members—utilize the two R's and/or immortality as
their basis. Relatively infrequent is any further affirmation.

There is an area of silence, however, which corresponds precisely to the most poignant concern of the typically bereaved
person. The really important question is just this: Will he go
on as a person? Will I see him again? The other things said at
the time of bereavement, whether with religious words ("eternal
life," "immortality") or not, whether with specificity or not (for
example, reference to the deceased's good qualities or good
deeds to be remembered), or whether by clergymen or laymen,
range from platitudes to sensitive recall. If in fact there is
nothing more which can be responsibly and honestly affirmed,
then we should be glad both that this much, which can easily
be said, is in fact said in so many cases, and also that no more is
said. Honesty, integrity, and respect for the bereaved require
silence as to what cannot be affirmed. Pious—even if well-

meaning—fraud is the violation of a person, even if at a time of crisis he might appear to receive some comfort from it.

On the other hand, if there is something which can be legitimately affirmed and which touches the really significant question, then it ought to be said. A reassuring positive answer is important if it has a sound basis, especially when its truth brings not only immediate comfort, but long-range hope based on quiet reflective analysis.

The Fear of Death

The phenomenon of death and its inevitability is in every one's mind—although not so frequently in the conscious mind, because either we deliberately suppress it or our automatic processes keep it repressed—most of the time. But it is never far beneath the surface. Nor is the corollary: the fear of death.[2]

Not very profound reflection is required to perceive what it is that is actually feared. The fear of death in the more literal sense of the fear of *dying* has some specificable limits. It probably would rationally apply only to certain modes of death: seriously maiming accidents or forms of illness which bring great pain in the interim—whether for three minutes or for three months. There is obviously nothing to fear about the process of dying should it occur in one's sleep or be instantaneous. But there are no such limits to what is feared about death apart from dying itself. For many, it is *the fear of the absolute end of one's conscious existence as a person.* Conventional Christianity has a pre-fab answer to this fear. Whether the answer (in its varying forms, and on varying bases of authority) is plausible or not, there is no question concerning its relevance. And those of us who choose to make meaning-affirmations on another basis cannot dodge this issue.

Yet before approaching it we should take into account the fact that there are some people to whom this basic fear does not present itself in the form just stated. First, there are still some

[2] See the author's *Beyond Anxiety* (New York: Scribner's, 1953), Chap. 8.

people who have no conscious doubt (and perhaps this is true of the *unconscious* minds of a good many of us) about eternal life, but for whom the very authority-support for this certainty also involves belief in a real hell of infinite torment. For them this composite conviction is not entirely a comfortable one. Many of these persons carry unresolved guilt feelings which leave open for them the possibility that their abode in the life to come may be this very hell in which they believe. For these hapless persons belief in immortality carries with it the hope of eternal bliss, but also the fear of everlasting torture. So there are persons for whom belief in the life to come is more or less real, but for whom the fear of an eternal hell abides, either consciously or unconsciously.

Others, on the other hand, have personally gone through what many fundamentalists call "the Scheme of Salvation" (conviction of sin→justification by grace through faith→sanctification) or, in accordance with the convictions of the Pentecostalist groups, have experienced Surrender and the Second Baptism, and thus in their conscious minds at least are in possession of "the Blessed Assurance." Though the composite conviction of such believers is eternal life *cum* heaven, yet there is actually in practice considerable uneasiness—and not always submerged—as to whether "the real thing" has actually happened.[3]

A parallel is found in a tradition which in most respects is radically different. Until the recent Papal elimination of categories of indulgences and other earthly commitments regarding after–life outcomes, the Roman Catholic Church taught that any person who received Holy Communion in a state of grace for nine consecutive first Fridays of the month would be guaranteed ultimate entrance into heaven—no matter what happened in his earthly life thereafter. One would think that a modicum of efficiency with reference to one's date book and alarm clock could thus dispose of the fear of hell. But not so. The haunting

3 Paul Tournier, *Guilt and Grace,* translated Arthur W. Heathcote *et al.* (Toronto: Hodder & Stoughton, 1962), p. 154.

fear remains—and one grounded in a rational basis. How can one be sure that he was in fact in a state of grace on each and every one of those nine specified occasions? Was perhaps a mortal sin omitted in the recounting in the confessional box prior to one or more of those special Communions? Was genuine repentance always present? Might one have committed a mortal sin after Absolution and before receiving the Sacrament—perhaps an impure thought, written off at the time as without "sufficient reflection" or without "full consent of the will" when actually God might not have so adjudged the episode? Etc., etc.

In another staunch tradition, neither "sectarian" nor "Papist," namely, Calvinism, belief in the doctrine of Predestination is supposed to relieve the fear of hell for some, "the Elect." But how can one be absolutely sure that he is of this blessed company? Notably unsatisfactory (from a logical point of view) on the issue of Predestination are the Articles of Religion of semi-Calvinized Anglicanism. In fact the relevant Article in its studied ambiguity is one of the best examples of the politically influenced compromise known as the Elizabethan Settlement. Yet as an empirical description of the alternate states of mind of persons thinking about this subject, and of the resulting psychological effects, Article XVII is quite revealing:

As the godly consideration of Predestination, and our Election in Christ, is full of sweet, pleasant, and unspeakable comfort to godly persons, and such as feel in themselves the working of the Spirit of Christ, mortifying the works of the flesh, and their earthly members, and drawing up their mind to high and heavenly things, as well because it doth greatly establish and confirm their faith of eternal Salvation to be enjoyed through Christ, as because it doth fervently kindle their love towards God: So, for curious and carnal persons, lacking the Spirit of Christ, to have continually before their eyes the sentence of God's Predestination, is a most dangerous downfall, whereby the Devil doth thrust them either into desperation, or into wretchlessness of most unclean living, no less perilous than desperation.[4]

[4] What is above quoted is preceded by a fulsome, affirming description of "Predestination to Life," but there is omitted the other half of the Calvinist scheme of "double predestination," namely, predestination to

In an opposite category are those relatively few who seem quite convinced that death ends all and whose distaste for life is sufficient to cause them to take the initiative to move from something to nothing. Nowadays it is generally assumed that those who commit suicide have acted under uncontrollable compulsion or otherwise are mentally unbalanced. And there is an empirical basis for this generalization.[5] True, in the nature of the case, when unexpected suicidal action is successful, it is impossible to know precisely what was psychologically operative at the time of decision and action. But professional consultation with persons whose attempts were unsuccessful almost always reveals some pathology; the same is true of those taking their

---

eternal damnation. Then all that is said is hedged in a concluding paragraph referring the whole matter back to the Bible: "Furthermore, we must receive God's promises in such wise, as they be generally set forth to us in Holy Scriptures: and, in our doings, that Will of God is to be followed, which we have expressly declared unto us in the Word of God."

But this is only to confound ambiguity with contradiction. Cf. (1) "He destined us in love to be his sons through Jesus Christ, according to the purpose of his will" (Eph. 1:5); "In him, according to the purpose of him who accomplishes all things according to the counsel of his will" (Eph. 1:11); "though they were not yet born and had done nothing either good or bad, in order that God's purpose of election might continue, not because of works but because of his call" (Rom. 9:11); "And those whom he predestined he also called; and those whom he called he also justified; and those whom he justified he also glorified" (Rom. 8:30); "So too at the present time there is a remnant, chosen by grace" (Rom. 11:5); "For if their rejection means the reconciliation of the world, what will their acceptance mean but life from the dead?" (Rom. 11:15); and "they sing a new song before the throne and before the four living creatures and before the elders. No one could learn that song except the hundred and forty-four thousand who had been redeemed from the earth" (Rev. 14:3) (this precise number being important also to the Essenes and to the Jehovah's Witnesses); *with* (2) "And it shall be that whoever calls on the name of the Lord shall be saved" (Acts 2:21); "Therefore let any one who thinks that he stands take heed lest he fall" (1 Cor. 10:12); "and so all Israel will be saved; as it is written, 'The Deliverer will come from Zion, he will banish ungodliness from Jacob;'" (Rom. 11:26); "For God sent the Son into the world, not to condemn the world, but that the world might be saved through him" (John 3:17); and "You see that a man is justified by works and not by faith alone" (Jas. 2:24).

[5] James Hillman, PH.D., *Suicide and the Soul* (New York: Harper & Row, 1964), pp. 136–37.

lives whose psychological condition had previously been under observation, either in professional therapy or more informal counseling. And there are other, and by some cultural standards, even noble motives for suicide. For example, until recently there was sufficient religious and cultural indoctrination for a Hindu wife to find it appropriate to throw herself on her husband's funeral pyre or for a Japanese gentleman to choose hara-kiri over continued earthly existence with loss of face.

Nevertheless, for the majority of people, the image of death carries with it precisely what was stated earlier: the fear of the absolute end of one's conscious existence as a person. We may well find that there are plausible affirmations one can make which are relevant to the issues involved in the other attitudes described. But that possibility depends upon whether an adequate positive affirmation can be made with reference to this more fundamental fear.

An immediate barrier to any such affirmation, in any form, would seem to be the universally noticeable fact seemingly patent from straight observation, that when the body dies there is no more person. Ashes to ashes, and dust to dust.

The Extension of the Psyche

Earlier we have spelled out what is also universally noticeable, namely, that in any living person we have come to know there is the *more*, the beyond within, the transcendent and unique personality.[6] But there are more data than this. In our time scientific methods have been increasingly applied to a number of areas of perennial human experience which from the dawn of history have pointed to *the extension of the functioning of the person beyond the space-time continuum in which he is set*. The work of seriously considering such data and carefully drawing conclusions therefrom does not cast doubt upon the established positive truths of psychology nor on the conclusions about the

6 See pp. 92–94, above.

psychosomatic connection earlier discussed.[7] Rather, it represents the application of more reliable empirical processes to other aspects of reality about which heretofore the facts were scattered, inadequately evaluated, and mixed with superstition. Thus from a scientific point of view here is a new frontier and one of prime significance to those who would seek to make plausible affirmations about the meaning of persons and their destiny.

The dynamics of this whole development is analogous to the history of that now recognized, respectable, and ever more promising branch of science, nuclear physics. The medieval alchemists were convinced that the basic elements of the universe could be transmuted (for example, lead into gold). With the coming of the Age of Enlightment, the suppositions of the alchemists and their resultant methodology were definitely exploded by scientific observers (for whom Charles Dalton stands as the symbol) who distinguished the various elements and established them as the basic "building blocks" of the material of the universe—elements which, it appeared, could not be further subdivided or transmuted. This phase was necessary to "clean up the scene," discredit the elaborate but fruitless endeavors of the alchemists, and provide a workable basis for the flourishing of chemistry as a laboratory science and as a foundation for technological investigations. But while this process has gone on unabated and with increasingly fruitful effects, Einstein and his heirs had the courage to move on beyond the once respectable status quo to the frontier. Through imaginative thought, further gathering of data, and empirical testing, we were brought to an understanding and practice which, while not contradicting the limited conclusions of the older physics and chemistry, revealed that basic elements *do* transmute and that in fact we can do it ourselves (for weal and/or woe!).

So in the field with which we are here concerned. In all times and cultures, from the most primitive on, there have been alchemists of the spirit: those who generalized about, and sought

7 See pp. 90–92, above.

to systematize—and effect—the functioning of various real or apparent phenomena beyond the normal day-to-day experience of persons. These included visions and "voices"; prophetic predictions about future events; divine revelation not only of ideas but of specific words; possession by demons, and the exorcism thereof; apparitions of angels and of deceased persons; the appearance, disappearance, and movement of objects without physical intervention; raising up of the dead; mind-reading; the applying or ingesting of various "holy" substances for the purpose of achieving such extraordinary results as healing, ecstasy, and visions; speaking with strange tongues and the interpretation of tongues spoken; levitation; bilocation purportedly involving the separate but connected functioning of an "astral body"; and one- and two-way communications with the dead.

In this alchemy of the spirit, several common features tended to appear. First, a certain professionalism generally developed around one or more of these areas of phenomena. In some times and places there was an absolute exclusivism: only those admitted to the "union" were allowed to practice, it being taught or implied that others either couldn't or shouldn't.[8] In other times and places the occurrence of such phenomena apart from such specialists was not denied nor were attempts to induce them forbidden, but recognized was the existence of special gifts residing in certain individuals[9]—sometimes those officially admitted to a given guild, sometimes those who had simply gained a reputation for such aptitudes. Second, in both the professional and common understanding of these things, generally assumed—explicitly or implicitly—was a dualism between soul/spirit and body/flesh and, more specifically, the existence and action of disembodied spirits. Third, both theory and practice utilized another dichotomy: the natural and the

---

[8] E.g., "Exorcist" has from the earliest times been one of the "minor orders" of the Roman Catholic Church; but for many centuries further authorization (consent of the Bishop) has been required for them and those in higher orders to seek to drive out demons.

[9] Cf. 1 Cor. 12.

supernatural. Presupposed were planes of existence above and below the everyday world with its web of observable and predictable causal relationships.

Then from the Enlightenment on there increasingly developed a new kind of professional, one who disciplined himself to examine objectively the nature and operation of natural phenomena. On the one hand, he deliberately discarded anything not subject to empirical testing, and, on the other, he sought to extend the scope of phenomena to which such laboratory methods could be applied. The obvious success of this approach, both in the extension of reliable knowledge and in the invention and technological production of a multitude of devices which directly (and more or less reliably) have met specific needs and provided tangible comforts, almost completely diminished the need to utilize the various categories in earlier times associated with the "supernatural." One by one certain happenings—from earthquakes[10] to illnesses—hitherto attributed to the heavenly or demonic planes of existence, have been brought within the ambit of science. By no means is the process complete: there is obviously much yet unexplained. But the process has certainly gone far enough to have undermined the confidence in the category of the supernatural. Though we do not yet know fully what is and what isn't, or know fully the causes of all that undeniably is, we have reached the point where it is only sensible to grant that if something is, it is *natural*; if it isn't, it isn't made so by calling it supernatural.

With the development of science, attention was naturally paid first to the more obvious and predictably recurring material items. This preoccupation, vindicated by its fruitful results, actually tended to block the exploration into less external things not plainly visible. Those moving toward what was then a frontier were not at first accorded "scientific" status. Hence, the difficulty in securing recognition of psychology, anthropology,

10 A simple example: the discovery of the earthquake fault at the likely location of Sodom and Gomorrah, thought to have been destroyed by God for homosexuality (Gen. 19:24–25).

and sociology as legitimate sciences and the slowness with which psychiatry (apart from neurology) was accepted as an honorable medical specialty. The turgidity of such resistance represents a good thing: being affirmed were the exclusiveness of the natural, the sole legitimacy of the empirical method, and the primacy of fact. The history of the slow but eventual acceptance of the latter sciences makes these things clear: no longer, either in the ranks of professional sciences or among educated people, can an area of purported reality be taken seriously which claims to transcend the natural; no longer will an -ology be regarded as legitimate which does not proceed by the empirical method; and not for much longer will generic affirmations—no matter how long held, religiously or otherwise—receive general acceptance unless they can qualify as plausible inferences from established data.

But the fact is that these "new" sciences—not so long ago in history written off as pseudosciences—have been admitted to the family of respectable disciplines. Now, having met the tests which were the bases of the resistance to that recognition, the professionals in these newer fields are joined with those of the longer established sciences in an understandably conservative protectiveness of the purity of the scientific method in their attitude toward those who have begun to operate systematically in the investigation of an even newer frontier: the extended functioning of the human psyche.

A revealing symbol of both the moving out and the resistance is the title devised years ago for the purpose of the academic scene, when J. B. Rhine of Duke University began to pioneer in the empirical approach to extrasensory phenomena. The frontier endeavor was begun in the new "Department of Parapsychology." On a basis of the principles just considered, parapsychology ("beyond" psychology) is a nonword—or rather, a word for a nonconcept. Either there is reality to extrasensory phenomena or there is not. If there is, then it is a function of the human psyche, and its study is a part of *psych*ology; if there isn't there is nothing to have an -*ology* about. (Analogous would

be to call astrology "para-astronomy," or to call the endeavor to
to crack the genetic code "para-biochemistry." Fortunately, the
title given the institution where the more recent research work
of Dr. Rhine and his staff is conducted, though perhaps over-
generic, avoids the implication of unreality: the Institute for
the Study of Man.

Still common, on the part of both scientists and nonscientists,
is this reaction to any reported data or inferences from these
frontier psychological areas: It can't be so. Or: Whatever is
claimed as data *must* be explainable some other way; for example, coincidence, the psychological malfunctioning of the
witnesses, or the credulity of the experimenter.[11] Such responses
are of the same character as the reaction of sensible or respectable people in medieval times to the beginnings of what today
are the most taken-for-granted sciences (an ugly well-known
reaction in the case of Galileo, for example) and the later reaction of established scientists to what is now standard in psychology and psychiatry. Actually such a response is quite
unscientific. A careful critique of the reality of the purported
data, of the methods of experimentation, and of the connections
between what is verified and the conclusions inferred—in any
field, new or old—is quite in accord with the scientific spirit.
But an a priori declaration that something *can't* be so is dogma,
not science.

It is in this spirit that we know turn more specifically to some

11 The expression of this attitude, though beginning to wane, is so widespread (the author has found this from his personal experience of response
of this type on the part of some on occasions when he has spoken on the
subject in lectures and at conferences), special care has been taken in
the pages which follow to provide, through the footnotes, ample citations
to documentation and empirically approached analyses. Unlike other citations in the book the indication of the qualifications of most of the authors
has been included. Some will view this as being defensive—to which the
answer is, it *is*—and appropriately so in the light of what has been said
above; but it is not "name dropping," nor is it the reverting to an
"authority" basis for belief (cf. Chap. 4); precisely what is intended by
the indication of the scholarly qualifications of the authors and the specific
data described and analyzed in their books is to *neutralize* somewhat the
widespread bias referred to.

of the new areas of empirical investigation which appear to portray man as functioning, in the here and now certainly, but beyond the space-time continuum. A plausible basis for such a view of the psyche of living persons—if there be such—would, to say the least, have an important bearing on the credibility of any phenomena purporting to support an affirmation of the survival of persons beyond death. Suspending judgment about the soundness of data and conclusions regarding either the extension of the psyche now or personal survival after physical death, there are two important reasons for correlating reflection on the two fiields.

First, an empirical concern. If those aspects of human personality which we subsume under the label soul/spirit/psyche cannot be seen as transcending in any way the limits of the person's physical mechanism, then these "spiritual" aspects must be seen simply as a *function* of his physiological structure— automatically ceasing, therefore, when the organism dies. There would be nothing which *could* go on.

Second, a theological concern. If a person does not in this life already possess that which goes on, then the conferring of it upon him would require a special divine intervention in connection with each deceased person (or each of the selected ones who constitute the Elect). And this would require acceptance of a doctrine of Special Providence—which, as we shall see,[12] does not appear plausible. Moreover, if the given individual, including that which is essential to his unique person, does in fact die *in toto,* then, even such an activity within the category of Special Providence (if credible) would require that which is "resurrected" to be, by obvious logic, a new person and not the same person.

So it would appear important to evaluate the extent to which the human psyche would appear capable of transcending the time-space continum in the here and now as a basis for assessing the plausibility of an affirmation of survival after death. Either, by the nature and the function of the psyche, we participate *now*

[12] See pp. 171–73, below.

in "eternal life" (i.e., meaning that time and space do not bind us, but merely enable us to "measure" our present experiences) or there is no such thing. Further an "eternal life" which is conceived of as an unchanging status after death would seem to contradict the nature of our present experience, as we shall see below.

Extension of the psyche here and now *is* affirmable through data and hypotheses in a number of fields which have not always been seen as related, even by those who have given concentrated attention to one or another of them. But, fortunately for progress in perceiving the full scope of the functioning of the human psyche, there are many who are beginning to see the material in these several fields as pieces of a jigsaw puzzle which show some signs of falling together into what can be identified as a consistent design. In fact, there has come into more common "neutral" use a symbol to refer, in these fields, to that which is perceived beyond the ordinary expected limitations, i.e., the paranormal. It is ψ (psi). The growing recognition of the interconnection of these categories which have in recent times been moving into the realm of the empirical is important for two reasons: on the quantitative side the amount of verified data in some of these fields is relatively slender[13] as compared with the breadth of the data-base in disciplines which have been functioning scientifically for a longer time; and the plausibility of the ψ generic inferred from the data in any one of the fields gains strength from the degree of plausibility of the same inference from data in the other fields. Nevertheless, in spite of their new "ecumenism," some of these fields have had a separate development and have been getting at the matter from different directions.[14]

[13] "Don't disparage research just because it is based on a small number of cases. The size of sample needed depends on the nature of the problem, complexity of the analysis, and the character of the data." Leo Bogart, "How to Get the Most Out of Market Research," *Harvard Business Review*, January-February, 1956, Vol. 34, No. 1, p. 79.

[14] Excellent and detailed treatments, from an empirical approach, of most of the areas considered below (though not of glossalalia or psychedelic

Extrasensory Perception

Reference has already been made to empirical study of ESP.[15]
The first of these fields to undergo rigorous laboratory investigation was that of simultaneous communication or *telepathy*.
The phenomenon itself, sometimes called "mind-reading," has

---

phenomena, for which other references will be given) are *The Imprisoned Splendour* by the physicist Raynor C. Johnson, M.A. (Oxon), D.SC. (London), Master of Queen's College, University of Melbourne (New York: Harper & Row, 1953), with foreword by the Rev. Leslie D. Weatherhead, PH.D., D.D.; *The Supreme Adventure: Analyses of Psychic Communications,* by Robert Crookall, D.SC., PH.D., late Principal Geologist, H. M. Geological Survey, London (London: James Clarke & Co., 1961), with Introduction by the Rev. Canon John D. Pearce-Higgins, Vice-Provost of Southwark Cathedral; *Challenge of Psychical Research: A Primer of Parapsychology,* by Gardner Murphy, M.D., of the Menninger Foundation (New York: Harper & Row, 1961). Many cases in these fields are reported in *The Unexplained* by Allen Spraggett, minister and religion editor of the *Toronto Star* (New York: New American Library, 1967). A summary of many instances reported through correspondence due to knowledge of the laboratory work undertaken at Duke University under the direction of her husband, Dr. J. B. Rhine, and analysis of the reports in the light of this experimental program is provided in *Hidden Channels of the Mind,* by Louisa E. Rhine, PH.D., now with the Institute for the Study of Man, Durham, N. C. (New York: William Sloan Associates, 1961). Psychological and philosophical analyses of data in these fields, along with reports of many of his own experiences, are given by the late Dr. C. G. Jung in *Memories, Dreams, Reflections,* edited by Aniela Jaffé (New York: Vintage Books, Random House, 1961).

15 For a survey of the field, its methods of research, and the results of experiments, see *Parapsychology: Frontier Science of the Mind,* by J. B. Rhine, PH.D., and J. G. Pratt, PH.D. (Springfield, Ill.: Charles C. Thomas, 1957). See also *ESP and Personality Patterns,* by G. R. Schmeidler and R. A. McConnell (New Haven: Yale University Press, 1958), a joint account by a psychologist and a physicist; *Modern Experiments in Telepathy,* by S. G. Saol, PH.D., formerly Lecturer in Pure Mathematics, University of London, and F. Bateman (New Haven: Yale University Press, 1954), a survey of English research; *Sense and Nonsense in Psychology,* by the psychologist H. J. Eysench, PH.D. (Baltimore: Penguin Books, 1957), Chap. 3; *Telepathy and Medical Psychology,* by the psychiatrist Jan Ehrenwald, M.D. (New York: W. W. Norton, 1948); and the quarterly issues of the *Journal of Parapsychology* (Durham, N. C.: Duke University Press), founded in 1937 and reporting original research, discussions, book reviews, and abstracts of current research in other periodicals.

been thought to have been experienced at one time or another by a good proportion of the population. But except in the case of a relatively few professional mind-readers (the best of whom have rarely qualified as scientists either in stature or methodology, and the worst of whom have been viewed as charlatans), individual experience was not sufficiently consistent or centrally collated to provide an adequate empirical base. However, since the pioneering work of Dr. Rhine various centers throughout the world over the years have provided a broad data base in the testing, under controlled laboratory conditions, of the ability of individual persons to communicate directly with one another *in absentia* and without visual, aural, mechanical, electrical, electronic, or magnetic modes of contact.

The bulk of the experiment consists of the attempted transmission or reception of a few standardized symbols. In this regard the experimentation is analogous to laboratory work in physics where the individual units are controlled,[16] as contrasted with experiments for the purpose of categorization in, for example, most areas of psychology and sociology. On the other hand, the work bears a similarity to the latter in that there is obviously a high degree of differentiation between the receptive subjects chosen for the experiments. But, as in these latter fields, the large quantitative factor compensates for the differentiation.

As in any other scientific field, there are schools of thought regarding the most appropriate modes of testing and setting up of controls and mutual critique of various systems which have been in operation. But the results, by and large, display a percentage of correlation between what is in the mind of the transmitters and what is in the mind of the recipients which is well above what would be called for by the law of probabilities. Precisely this correlation is the pointer to the existence of ψ.

[16] As early as 1940 Dr. Rhine and his associates were able to report the results of 142 separate projects of parapsychological research, involving more than 3,600,000 trials. More than 60 per cent of the studies had been made elsewhere than Duke. *Extra-Sensory Perception after Sixty Years* (New York: Henry Holt, 1940).

Extensive experimentation has been undertaken in regard to the perception from a distance, not of the thoughts of another person, but of inanimate objects—*clairvoyance*. Similar results ensue: a higher degree of correct perception than called for by the law of probabilities. Random and unstructured instances of this type of experience on the part of individuals provide too narrow an empirical base from which to draw convincingly a generic which would earn general conviction; yet they are consonant with the results drawn by the more disciplined empirical method.

As in the case of telepathy and clairvoyance, many individuals throughout history and today have had distinct experiences of *precognition* or *retrocognition*. As real as these may have seemed to those experiencing such phenomena, the drawing of any conclusion which can be taken seriously had to await the application of the same methodology of laboratory experimentation used for contemporaneous perception or another's mental images and of material objects. What was lacking until recently was the staging of a uniform context for the recording of instances of pre– and retrocognition. Now that such has been developed, the results? The differential between positive indications and what would be "normal" under the law of probabilities, in cases of experiments involving perception beyond *both* space and time limitations, turns out—as would be expected—to be smaller than in the case of those involving only transcendence of space. Nevertheless, the studies reflect that this differential is a pointer to the reality of ψ. As in the case of simultaneous reception, private experiences of the given type receive a certain standing as additional items of data in the light of the scientific experimentation.

Psychedelic Phenomena

Research and discovery in the fields of anthropology and the history of religions have established that connected with most primitive religions has been the use of one or another of the many psychedelic drugs as part of the sacramental rites of the cult. This has been found to be true of various American Indian tribes and of the primitive stages of Oriental religions. Too, there is some reason to think that the oil of anointing[17] and shew bread[18] of primitive Judaism was psychedelic in nature. And now one of the prominent developments our times has been the discovery (or rediscovery) of a variety of conscious-ness-expanding drugs[19] and the rapid increase in their use by individuals, alone or in groups, in an explicitly religious context or apart from such.[20] Many persons have been able to describe their "trips" and articulate to a degree the meaning such trips have had for them—whether on LSD, psybocilin, a species of Mexican mushroom, mescaline, peyote, romilar,[21] marijuana, or hashish.[22]

In recent years there have been established in various locali-ties a number of institutional programs for experimentation and research in this field, some with therapy as the main objective[23] (some individual psychiatrists also have been using such drugs therapeutically), and others in the interest of providing a broad enough empirical base for drawing some conclusions about the nature of the human psyche. It is unfortunate that the recent widespread scare about the use of psychedelic drugs, especially LSD (a scare which is by no means entirely paranoid, since it

[17] Exod. 30:23–33.

[18] Num. 4:3–15.

[19] For reports of experiences and analyses see Sydney Cohen, *The Be-yond Within* (New York: Atheneum Press, 1964); Aldous Huxley, *Doors of Perception* and *Heaven and Hell* (New York: Harper & Row, 1954 and 1956); and Alan Watts, *Joyous Cosmology* (New York: University Books, 1962).

[20] E.g., Dr. Timothy Leary's "League for Spiritual Discovery" (abbreviated LSD!). Cf. *People* v. *Woody*, 61 Cal. (2d) 716 (1964), in which it was ruled that the "free exercise of religion" clause in the First Amendment to the Constitution protected the right of an Indian cult to continue its long-standing sacramental use of peyote despite the prohibition of the State's criminal code.

[21] Not strictly speaking psychedelic, but productive of similar results.

[22] The latter two are not in the category of psychedelic drugs nor is their use accompanied by the same dangers (in fact they are less potentially harmful than alcohol), but their use can be the catalyst for inner experi-ences like some facets of psychedelic phenomena.

[23] Notably the extensive—and markedly successful—program for the treatment of alcoholics, in the Province of Saskatchewan.

is increasingly evident that the unsupervised use of such drugs involves a number of explicit dangers which are increasingly definable and understandable), while apparently not reducing the consumption of such drugs in an undisciplined and unprofessional way, has nevertheless considerably restricted the scientific exploration. It is to be hoped—even assumed—that in due time the latter will pick up again, and indeed be increased in breadth and scope.

In the light of the present uncertainty about psychedelics and for its own value in the rounding out of the picture, it is good that experimentation has proceeded in the creation of a nonchemical context for psychedelic experience. A project in the Department of Psychiatry at the University of California Medical School in San Francisco has achieved positive results through a procedure utilizing a Pavlovian method of inducing a pattern or response. The subject sits in a totally dark chamber. His head is wired to a recording apparatus which indicates throughout the course of the experiment the rise and fall of the rate of the α-cycle in the brain—the results depending on the degree to which the subject's mind is "empty" of concentration on thoughts. Whenever the α-wave line on the graph hits a certain "low" (e.g., eight cycles per second) a bell sound rings softly inside the chamber, providing the subject with an immediate sign of achievement and contributing markedly to his capacity to maintain the optimum state. For example, in one case, reported to the author immediately after the conclusion of the experiment, an experience with a visionary component began within three quarters of an hour. And, incidentally, the particular dynamic pattern of imagery matched identically an experience described to the author a few months before by another person who had used LSD.

Mystical Experience

Ecstatic experiences such as those experienced under drugs or in the experiments just described have generally come to mystics after long periods of withdrawal and discipline. Sometimes such efforts have also been accompanied by sustained fasting—and it may very well be that the somatic alterations resulting therefrom have a direct bearing on the psychic receptivity, as in the case of drugs. In other cases[24] experiences just "come" unexpectedly without special efforts toward such an end. But the fact that experiences ensue from the use of different drugs or the use of various regimens of mental "emptying," accompanied or unaccompanied by physical deprivations or bodily actions or disciplined physical inaction, or simply as "gift" to receptive spirits, confirms a well-founded thesis that the use of drugs does not *cause* the phenomena, but rather only suspends the functioning of that portion of the brain, which normally blocks or screens—doubtless mercifully[25]—what otherwise would be an ever-present openness to such apprehensions of broader reality.

Experiments in consciousness-expansion of the type described above are focusing attention again upon the self-disclosures of such mystics in the Western tradition as the seventeenth-century St. Theresa of Avila and St. John of the Cross, and of mystics in the Oriental traditions—especially those who have adopted the methods of the Zen masters. Also being reread with new understanding are analyses such as that of Professor William James in his *Varieties of Religious Experience*,[26] and collations are being made of writings in other times and cultures on religious experience (or "peak experience," as it is called by Professor Abraham Maslow[27]—a useful phrase, since some such are accompanied by religious symbols and some are not), such as the recent analysis by Professor E. R. Dodds of descriptions of

24 See Richard M. Bucke, *Cosmic Consciousness* (New Hyde Park, N. Y.: University Books, 1961).

25 There is an hypothesis that a factor in some cases of paranoia is the lack of an adequate filtering process in the given individual.

26 The Gifford Lectures for 1901–1902 (London and Glasgow: Fontana Library, 1960).

27 *Religion, Values, and Peak-Experiences* (Athens, Ohio: Ohio University Press, 1965).

such phenomena by pagan and Christian writers in the Roman Empire in the period from Marcus Aurelius to Constantine.[28]

Plotinus, the second-century Neo-Platonist, to give just one example, speaks of a number of occasions:

I awakened out of the body into myself and came to be external to all other things and contained within myself, when I saw a marvelous beauty and was confident, then if ever, that I belonged to the higher order, when I actively enjoyed the noblest form of life, when I had become one with the Divine and stabilized myself in the Divine.[29]

Apparently such experiences come by no conscious act of the will: Plotinus says, "we must wait quietly for its appearance and prepare ourselves to contemplate it, as the eye waits for the sunrise."[30] And description of the consummation seems difficult. But here is one of Plotinus' attempts:

The soul sees God suddenly appearing within it, because there is nothing between: they are no longer two, but one; while the presence lasts, you cannot distinguish them. It is that union which earthly lovers imitate when they would be of one flesh. The soul is no longer conscious of being in a body, or of itself as having identity—man or living being, thing or sum of things. . . . For who it is that sees it has no leisure to see. When in this state the soul would exchange its present condition for nothing in the world, though it were offered the kingdom of all the heavens: for this is the Good, and there is nothing better.[31]

Descriptions of the same purport have been essayed by persons of widely varying religious and philosophical orientations, by persons who had been conditioned for the experience with or without drugs, and by using a variety of methods in either case. Several common features can be noted, which are manifest to different degrees in different phases of reported experiences:

a. The person discovers that innate in man is a greater

[28] *Pagan and Christian in an Age of Anxiety* (Cambridge, England: Cambridge University Press, 1965).
[29] *Op. cit.*, IV, iv, viii, 1.1 ff. (Henry and Schwizzer, eds.).
[30] *Ibid.*, v, 8.3.
[31] *Ibid.*, VI, vii, 34.12 ff.; see also VI, ix, 10–11.

capacity for conscious awareness of his environment than is exercised in his "normal" day-to-day existence. Even the corporeal opaqueness of material things can disappear or be modified.[32]

b. There can be awareness of two "selves," a vividly experiencing self and an observing self, the first uninterruptedly "lost" in the mystical state, the other making rational decisions and performing customary actions.[33]

c. Time and space can be suspended as a category of reality, such suspension being concurrent with full—indeed heightened —consciousness.[34]

d. As in two acts of a play, often there can be a desparate sense of utter isolation and separation from all things and a glorious sense of personal identification with God/the All/the One.

e. As part of the drama, there can appear pictorial episodes which represent locales and/or past historical periods with which the subject is familiar or with which he is definitely not. Also there can appear archetypal images, ones either consonant with the subject's own religious background or ones which are not, and of which the subject has never had conscious knowledge, e.g., from ancient and primitive religions of different cultures. Too, images can appear which have relevance to the primitive people who have long used a particular drug; for example, the recurrence of "the big cats" in the imagery of subjects given Yahee, which has been used for 1500 years by an Indian tribe in the Chilean Andes—where such species abound, even when the cats are not part of the environment of users.

These common features in the experiences and visions hap-

[32] Cf. *ibid.*, VI, vii, 21.25 ff., and VI, ix, 9.39.

[33] This apparent duality (it is actually identified today in connection with psychedelic experimentation as a temporary schizophrenia—the word not used in this connection in a pejorative sense) is not noted in the illuminating passage quoted from Plotinus, but is implicit in the very fact of his *awareness* of the sense of loss of identity and his capacity subsequently to describe it.

[34] *Ibid.*

pening under various methods seem to point to a generic quality in episodes of consciousness expansion, whether drug-induced or not. Dodds concludes, that what has "been described again and again, from ancient India to modern America, and in much the same terms . . . is recognizably the same psychological experience everywhere, however different the glasses that have been put upon it, however incompatible the theologies which it has been held to confirm.[35]

Throughout history and varying cultures, as Professor Dodd's statement implies, there has been a well-nigh universal tendency toward unreflective over-belief in connection with instances of specific religious experience. If the subject is already a member of a particular Church with a set of official beliefs, an astonishing spiritual episode is more often than not seen by the one experiencing it as absolute verification of the given Church's whole system of belief. If the subject has been an "unbeliever" but the human catalyst of the experience (for example, an evangelist or healer) is a representative of a particular Church, then the same result can ensue: the subject sees the personal experience as divine endorsement of the middleman's system of belief.

Sometimes more selective results occur. For example, Bernadette of Lourdes said her prayers regularly before a life-sized statue of Mary in her parish church. At this time there was much discussion in the Roman Catholic Church about whether Mary was immaculately conceived, that is, without taint of original sin. Both the proponents and opponents of the notion were quite vocal—and with feeling—right down to the grass-roots level. Her own pastor was on the side of the "higher" Mariology. One day at a site near the village she experienced a vision of Mary standing at the top of a grotto. Not surprisingly, the visage and attire closely resembled the statue of Mary in the church. In addition, she experienced seeing across the bottom of the figure an inscription reading in French, I AM THE IMMACULATE CONCEPTION. For her, for those with whom she shared the experience, and for the multitudes who learned of it through

[35] *Op. cit.*, n. 18, p. 86.

increasingly wide publicity, verification was seen for one side of the debate, the side which in fact received official—indeed infallible—establishment with the declaration of Pope Pius IX in 1854. Most unbelievers and Protestants[36] (those who have thought about the matter at all) have rejected the entire story as illusory (or in the case of those of more anti-Papist proclivities, contrived). But actually such an undiscriminating rejection is in itself dogmatic and a form of over-belief. Three elements in the account need to be distinguished.

First, there is no reason to assume, a priori, that Bernadette did not have an actual, datable inner experience.

Second, as to the form of the apparition, a rather commonplace explanation is available: it can plausibly be assumed that it represented a projection from the unconscious mind, and the source of the image thoroughly and repeatedly introjected into the unconscious mind was a real thing, namely, a particular statue of Mary in the parish church.

On still a third level, however, is the conceptual content of the experience (as indicated by its accompanying inscription). Here we have a precise example of the category of over-belief. For example, there is no reason to suppose that if the pastor had been repeatedly expressing himself on the *other* side of the question, which was then still open in the Roman Catholic Church, the inscription might not have read I AM NOT THE IMMACULATE CONCEPTION. In short, recognition of the fact that the particular

---

[36] The objection, prior to the Papal declaration, to this position by many Roman Catholic scholars and the rejection of it on the part of non-Roman Catholics (except for some Anglo-Catholics in the Anglican Communion) is understandable insofar as the rejectors have believed in the Doctrine of Original Sin. Granting this conviction about mankind generally, there appears to be no basis in Scripture, tradition, logic, or data for exempting Mary. But for those—including many now in the Roman Catholic Church (e.g., see the new Catechism issued by the Dutch hierarchy, which does not affirm this traditional doctrine as applicable to anyone's conception)—there is no reason to cavil at the affirmation "Mary was conceived without sin." So were the author and his readers. In this we are in good company: cf. the affirmation about Jesus' conception intoned in the Anglican Proper Preface for the Christmas octave: "And that without spot of sin . . ." (*Book of Common Prayer*, p. 77).

inner experience does not prove or disprove the doctrinal view, and explanation of the image not as a person actually standing at the head of the grotto (photographable, etc.), but as a subjective phenomenon understandable in terms of an objective source of introjection—these two things say nothing one way or the other as to whether a genuine peak-experience occurred. *Per contra*, the numerous instances of religious experience, in all times and places, taken along with the lack of any data which would suggest that Bernadette "made it up," would make it seem more than likely that a genuine experience did occur.

In the case of Bernadette's experience the imagery seem explainable in terms of factors in her conscious and unconscious mind. Other experiences seem to involve factors not thus traceable. In both dreams and mystical visions (whether made possible by chemistry or a regime of contemplation or "staging"[37]) elements have been included which have seemed excludable from the individual's personal history, excludable from the likely "intake" of his conscious or unconscious mind.[38] And this is particularly evident in a form of religious experience to which we now turn.

Glossolalia

In glossolalia,[39] or speaking with tongues, there emerges *through* the individual's unconscious mind, but apparently not *from* it, languages which have not been part of the experience or learning process of the speaker. There have been reported instances of speaking in known languages (either in their modern form or in a more archaic form) which are unknown to the speaker but understood by a listener who is competent in the given language. More commonly, that which is uttered though

[37] E.g., through the α-cycle methodology discussed on p. 130, above.
[38] See p. 138, below.
[39] For a comprehensive and objective treatment of this phenomenon see Morton T. Kelsey, *Tongue Speaking: An Experiment in Spiritual Experience* (Garden City, N.Y.: Doubleday, 1964). See also John L. Sherrill, *They Speak with Other Tongues* (New York: McGraw-Hill, 1964).

not an identifiable language has a "shape" which listening philologists have seen as justifying the conclusion that what is actually a language is being spoken. In short, glossolalia is not just babbling.

Associated with glossolalia is a correlative phenomenon: the "interpretation of tongues"[40] by persons who appear to be thus specially gifted. The "translations" of such an interpreter often are expressed in a way which is quite foreign to his customary mode of expression. Furthermore, what is reported as the meaning generally corresponds in content to the categories of discourse into which the speaker senses that his words fall. And, finally, with all the differences in personality, acculturation, education, environment, and location, two or three generic themes serve to classify most of what is thought, both by speakers in tongues and interpreters of tongues, to be the content of the words: adoration, thanksgiving, and joy. For that reason the most readily available literary analogues are those Biblical Psalms which fall in these categories and psalms which have more recently come to light, namely, the Songs of Thanksgiving in the Dead Sea Scrolls.

Tongue-speakers who are Christians attribute the experience to the direct action of the Holy Spirit, often referring to their initial experience of glossolalia as "the Baptism of the Holy Spirit" or "the Second Baptism." Further, usually they regard the experience as verifying conventional Christology, a literal eschatology, and a fundamentalist biblicism. But, quite apart from the soundness or unsoundness of these doctrinal positions as judged by other norms, the assumption of their truth on a basis of the fact of speaking in tongues is a case of over-belief. For the phenomenon of glossolalia has displayed itself all through history in quite diverse cultures and among people of quite diverse religious convictions.

Students of the subject who have sought to be objective, that is, open to accepting the reality of phenomena and, at the same time, wary of over-belief and inquisitive as to the psychological

40 E.g., I Cor. 12:10b.

dynamics involved in the process, have suggested as plausible a linkage to one or both of two other psychological categories. One is extrasensory perception: the subject's unconscious mind may be receiving what projects itself into speech from the unconscious or conscious mind of another person knowing the given language. But this explanation has its limitations. First, the speaking of known languages is the least common version of the phenomenon. Moreover, if it is assumed that the human transmitting station is a member of some remote and unknown tribe, while it can be granted that geographical distance has not proven a barrier to the functioning of telepathy, nevertheless this interpretation of cause-and-effect would involve an exceptionally selective instance of ESP. Finally, whether in the rarer instances of speaking in known languages or in the more common instances of utterances in unknown tongues, lacking still would be an hypothesis to explain of the content of what is spoken is usually limited (apart from instances of "prophecy") to praise, thanks, and exultation.

The "Group Unconscious"; Synchronicity

The second category suggested is the collective unconscious.[41] It is principally due to the late Dr. C. J. Jung of Zürich that there has been increasing recognition of the likelihood that there can come into the conscious arena material not only from the individual's unconscious mind but also from a deeper level sometimes called the "group unconscious." (A crude but clarifying analogy: one drilling for oil on a 100-foot lot will before long be pumping up oil from a wider pool underlying far more than his own terrain.) The supporting data for such a construct is the surfacing in persons of thoughts, images, and espe-

---

[41] See Jolan Jacobi, *The Psychology of Jung*, with foreword by the latter (New Haven: Yale University Press, 1943); Jung, *op. cit.* (n. 14, above); and Jung, *Psychological Types*, trans. by H. G. Baynes (London: Kegan Paul, 1933), pp. 616 ff.

cially archetypal symbols[42] which cannot seem to be accounted
for in a subject's own intake during his own life span. The
ultimate projection of this hypothesis would imply that in theory
(though by no means in common practice, due to the manifold
blocks to full awareness amply demonstrable with regard to the
individual conscious mind) everyone could be in touch with
everything that has ever been known or thought.[43] But one
would not have to make so universal an assertion to attribute
reality to that to which the collective unconscious category
points and for which there have been considerable supporting
data. However, to the extent that the group unconscious may
plausibly be viewed as the (or *a*) source of tongue-speaking,
there is a complication. What is thought to be said includes
reference to holy persons and places which are part of the religious acculturation of the speaker. This would imply that there
is some process by which unconsciously the tongue speaker is
utilizing a language unknown to him as a medium of expressing
things which are known to him, but not necessarily known to
the original speakers of the language.

The concept of the group unconscious, quite apart from its
usefulness in providing a possible explanation for glossalalia,
is in itself another pointer to the extension of the individual
psyche beyond the space-time continuum. It is consistent with
this broader implication that Dr. Jung took seriously the ancient
Chinese *Book of Changes*, the *I Ching*.

This remarkable collection of holy writings is thought to be

42 See *The Springs of Creativity: The Bible and the Creative Process of
the Psyche*, by the British psychologist, H. Westman (New York: Atheneum, 1961); and *Lord of the Four Quarters*, by the San Francisco psychiatrist, John Perry, M.D. (New York: George Braziller & Co., 1966).

43 "Today some of us believe (while others do not) that among the most
elusive and yet the most precious heirlooms of all were shadowy, deep-
seated memories of the experience of the evolving animal line during the
vast stretches of its history, memories which enrich and unite modern men
by throwing up from the unconscious the images and ideas that inspire
our arts and help to make them universally evocative." Jacquetta Hawkes
and Sir Leonard Woolley, *Prehistory and the Beginnings of Civilization*,
Vol. I of *History of Mankind, Cultural and Scientific Development*, spon-
sored by UNESCO (New York: Harper & Row, 1963).

the earliest recording of man's effort to place himself in relationship to the cosmos. It has been known in written form continuously to Oriental scholars since the fourth century B.C., although Chinese literature places the earliest authorship with Fu Hsi, a legendary character of such antiquity as to antedate historical memory—possibly of the era of the invention of cooking.[44] While it is generally agreed that this work forms the basis of two great philosophies, the Taoist and the Confucianist, the book itself is remarkably free of dogma—being simply a book of ethical wisdom which offers its guidance to a reader in need of help in any conceivable life situation. It has been dismissed by some readers, both Oriental and Western, as a book of oracles; but, as countless careful users of it throughout its long history have found, it works with uncommon accuracy. Dr. Jung studied the writing for thirty years before preparing his foreword to the Wilhelm edition and from this study formulated the principle of *synchronicity*. This remarkable theory of reality represents the most basic of empirical approaches; but Dr. Jung agrees it is only an attempt to make clear to the Western mind, trapped in a dualistic cause-effect frame of reference, the Chinese outlook on the universe in which the psyche exists as a component of a given situation. "The jumble of natural laws constituting empirical reality holds more significance for him [the Chinese Sage] than an equal explanation of events that, moreover, must equally be separated from one another in order to be properly dealt with."[45] Thus the words coincidence/luck/chance are found to be treated in a serious manner and can no longer stand for a comfortable dismissal of evidence of any kind.

In the last decade with the "shrinking" of our planet, and the ease (mechanically, at least) of the interchange of ideas, Zen Buddhist thought has become better known in the United States than previously was the entire two-and-one-half-millennia his-

44 *The I Ching,* the Richard Wilhelm Translation, translated by Carl F. Baynes, Bollingen Series XIX (New York: Pantheon Books, 1920), from the Introduction by Richard Wilhelm, p. xxxviii.
45 *Ibid.,* Foreword, p. iii.

tory of Buddhism—even when filtered through the dark glass of Western dualistic ontologies. The analogies between the development of Christian thought and Buddhist thought have always seemed remarkable, even though developments in Buddhism generally preceded those in Christianity. It is always somewhat startling to read in an encyclopedic or historical account of the springing up of the various Buddhist denominations, a paraphrase of a sentence such as this: In the twelfth century the Shin sect gave up ascetic practices, allowed its priests to be married, removed the inhibition against eating meat by the laity and priests, and insisted on the doctrine of salvation by faith rather than through good works.[46] With slight effort Zen can be seen as the New Theology of Buddhism which anticipated some centuries of Western thought and experience—certainly those of the group unconscious and the syncronistic.

Examples of the extension of the human psyche, such as those discussed in this chapter, are legion and of interest to the Zen Master only incidentally and sometimes negatively. As we have seen, the Daltonian view of the structure of elements and atoms needed to be viewed as an ultimate explanation of the workings of chemistry and physics before the scientific culture could move on to the principle of uncertainty and the modern science of astrophysics. In a similar way the principles of causality and acausality, the acceptance of psychic phenomena, and the experiences of mysticism need to be understood, surmounted—and then reaccepted in a different way by the Zen Buddhist seeking the desired "Enlightenment" or *satori*.[47]

This Eastern religion, with its high emphasis on the experiential and its insistence that ultimate truth cannot be reduced to words, nonetheless has accumulated a wonderful literature that serves as a guide to the seeker for truth but never is represented

[46] See, for example, a no more esoteric source than the *Encyclopaedia Britannica*, 1957, Vol. XII, p. 955.

[47] *The Three Pillars of Zen Teaching, Practice, and Enlightenment*, compiled and edited, with translation, introduction, and notes, by Philip Kapleau (New York: Harper & Row, 1966), pp. 38–41.

as a finalization of that truth.[48] It is obvious, and intended, that no explanation of this brief dialogue in the footnote can be given. It is just as obvious to the Zen Master, and desired by him, that the words be understood. The digestion and assimilation of this paradox/nonparadox can be a vehicle toward spiritual insight. *Kenosis,* self-emptying, leads to self-fulfillment. The entire range of experiences of the extension of the psyche eventually will lead to the viewing of such a simple act as eating as being totally in communion with the All while remaining a rational simple act.

Suzuki summarizes the chief characteristics of *satori* as (1) Irrationality; (2) Intuitive insight; (3) Authoritativeness (i.e., of the experience); (4) Affirmation; (5) Sense of the Beyond; (6) Impersonal Tone (i.e., highly intellectual); (7) Feeling of Exaltation; and (8) Momentariness.[49] It can be suspected that questions of the extension of the human psyche, when put to the Zen Master, might elicit one of three responses: a compassionate glance; an attitude of indifference; or a sharp rap across the knuckles. Hopefully, it would be the latter. Acausality–synchronicity.

Psychokinesis and Telekinesis

Before turning to the final category of evidence of communication with the dead it would be valuable to consider a phenomenon which is associated as frequently with the living as with the dead. In the terminology that has grown over the years in connection with paranormal events it is known by two names: *psychokinesis,* "the action of mind upon matter," and *telekinesis,*

---

48 In Suzuki's dispassionate, but beautiful writings, he describes the attainment of *satori* biographically; e.g., comprehension of the following is indicative of the nearness of *satori.* "A monk once asked Joshu, 'All things return to the One, but where does the One return?' To which the master answered, 'When I was in the province of Seiju . . . I had a monkish garment made which weighed seven kin.' " *Zen Buddhism, Selected Writings of D. T. Suzuki,* edited by William Barrett (Garden City, N.Y.: Doubleday, 1956), p. 100.

49 *Ibid.,* pp. 103–8.

"action at a distance," both referring to the movement of objects through space without physical agency. The former term is customarily used when only living persons are involved and the later when the phenomenon appears to be connected with a deceased person.

Psychokinesis has been subjected to rigorous laboratory experimentation with the most careful attention paid to objectivity of scientific conditions and the elimination of human error or fraud. Once it was established that objects could be moved without the intervention of any known physical means, two counter hypotheses for the occurrence of the recorded happenings were given. "Chance" (although this has no clear meaning in view of Jung's work on the principle of synchronicity) was the favored response on the part of those who chose to deny flatly the implications of the high scores. "Chance" results were then guarded against with great ingenuity by researchers at Duke University and the University of Pittsburgh, but the same pattern of results continued. The other explanation for the happenings was put forth by the researchers themselves and drawn from another, and older, well documented study of psychic phenomena, that of precognition. The experiments were then structured in a way to preclude this possible explanation and the same high scores obtained.[50]

Telekinesis, while less scientifically validated, has nonetheless gathered to it a large literature with much evidence of careful observation and recording by thoroughly reputable people. It is considered by those who witness it to be one of the most convincing of all psychic phenomena. One student of communication with the dead was a skeptic even though he had received in the company of others much evidence of purported communication with a deceased priest. Because he had a mental reservation, he refused to acquiesce in the reliability of the evidence, waiting for "a sign" which was to be the transportation from his apartment of one of four objects marked and known

[50] Rhine and Pratt, *op. cit.* (n. 15, above), pp. 59–65; Murphy, *op. cit.* (n. 14, above), Chap. 6, and other works cited in these two notes.

only to him. In the middle of one such conversation (through a medium) the priest suddenly announced that he would bring to the gathering one of the four objects. This object was a green enameled ash tray which dropped from a height of several feet and hit the hand of the subject. When he returned to his apartment he found the place occupied by that ash tray vacant.[51] This is offered simply as one example of typical situations reported by numerous investigators in many countries and times.

Psychic Phenomena

It has not been assumed in this brief discussion of a number of areas relating to the human personality which are beyond or on the edges of what had been the conventional borders of scientific disciplines that the data apparently available (and the amount of data varies considerably from area to area) or conclusions which have been drawn therefrom would supply an adequate empirical basis for inferring such transcendence by the human psyche of its apparent limitations as would be requisite for the affirmation of human survival beyond death. Nor has it been thought that available data and inferences from all these areas (and similar ones not covered) taken together actually prove such a conclusion.

The author's objective has been much more modest. It is twofold. First, these reminders of the existence of such phenomena and of plausible theories about them should rebut an all too common dogmatism (not the least among secularist-minded persons who claim to be free of dogmas) which would arbitrarily exclude even the possibility of a wider dimension of personal existence. Second, all such data and inferences about particular categories of these phenomena, when taken together provide a quite extensive base (and one growing more extensive all the time and with ever better methods of verification) for a view of the human psyche which would be consistent with posi-

51 Sherwood Eddy, *You Will Survive After Death* (Evanston: Clark Publishing Co., 1950), pp. 190–93.

tive data which point directly to personal survival. Even the best-supported claims of communication with deceased persons could hardly seem credible if seen as "out of the blue" and apart from the wider and variegated context of the extended functioning of the psyche which has just been summarized. Indeed, "neither will they be convinced if someone should rise from the dead!" If the respective areas adverted to are seen as pieces of a jigsaw puzzle which are beginning to appear to supply elements of an enlarged picture of the human psyche, then one would be ready at least to approach with some seriousness data from an area which, if reflecting reality, would supply the most singly significant piece of the puzzle.

Throughout human history, from earliest time down to the present, there have been reports of psychic phenomena. There has been a wide variety in the forms of narration; and associated with such stories—whether in official holy books or otherwise—has often been the assertion of various and conflicting doctrines about the after life. As has been pointed out above in other connections, over-belief can be involved. But as in these other categories, the inclusion of extrapolations in the report of an explicit experience neither proves or disproves what is extrapolated, nor automatically invalidates the reality of the reported experience.

The most conspicuous example (at least in Western civilization) of both the reports of psychic phenomena and the factors just analyzed is found in the Resurrection narratives in the New Testament.[52] Included are a number of firsthand and hearsay accounts of communication between Jesus after his death with various of his followers. Several decades elapsed before the writing of the accounts as we now have them (as compared with the "statute of limitations" of five years imposed by the British Society for Psychical Research); and the form of testimony, in some cases, suggests prior challenges to the oral narration. Therefore, it is not surprising that there are some contradictions among the reports: as to time, place, and percipients; as to the

[52] Mark 16:1–8; Matt. 28:1–10; Luke 24:1–9; John 20:1–18; Acts 1:1–9; I Cor. 15:4–8.

nature of the experience (there is a difference between an apparition in which a person is perceived as eating a fish and one in which he is perceived as walking through a closed door); and in the form of the messages reported as coming through.[53] Nevertheless, if on a broader empirical base it should be concludable that the phenomena which these narratives point to are in the category of reality *and* that deceased persons can be the source of them, one would not rule out, a priori, belief as to the ongoing life of Jesus and his being in contact with his disciples because of these variations in reporting and in interpretation. When it comes to various doctrines which the percipients and others believing in the reality of their experiences have regarded as being established by the phenomena, one must make a logical separation here with which we are already familiar.[54] The modern critic's or believer's view regarding one or another of the meanings affirmed as part of the account neither proves nor disproves the truth of the report of events; nor would the reality of the events establish the truth or relevance of any one of the reporters' meaning-affirmations.

With the foundation in 1822, by a group of distinguished leaders of British thought, of the Society for Psychical Research (followed in 1906 by the inauguration by William James and others of the American Society for Psychical Research), the age-old observation of such phenomena began to come within the ambit of scientific methodology.[55] It is impossible within the

[53] James McLeman, *Resurrection Then and Now* (London: Hodder & Stoughton, 1965).

[54] See pp. 49–50 and pp. 134–36, above.

[55] The literature is vast. Among the more useful surveys are *The Enigma of Survival*, by Hornel Hart, PH.D., for many years Professor of Sociology at Duke University; *A Critical Examination of the Belief in a Life After Death*, by C. J. Ducasse, PH.D., Professor of Philosophy, Emeritus, Brown University (Springfield, Ill.: Charles C. Thomas, 1961); *Beyond the Reach of the Sense*, by Rosalind Heywood (New York: Dutton, 1961); Crookall, *op. cit.* (n. 14, above); and Murphy, *op. cit.* (n. 14, above). See also Jung, *op. cit.* (n. 14, above). An exhaustive bibliography of books, monographs, and articles is furnished in Hart, *op. cit.*, pp. 264–76. Studies and analyses have been published over the decades in the *Proceedings of the Society for Psychical Research, Journal of the S.P.R.*, and *Journal of the American Society of Psychical Research*.

compass of this book to survey this whole field adequately. But
the author's conclusions from considerable reading and many interviews is substantially that carefully and comprehensively
stated by the late Sir Oliver Lodge, who had been President of
the British Association for the Advancement of Science and of
the Psychical Society of London, recipient of the Rumford Medal
of the Royal Society and of honorary degrees from Cambridge
and five other universities. He stated his position as follows:

Speaking for myself and with full and cautious responsibility, I
have to state that as an outcome of my investigations into psychical
matters I have at length and quite gradually become convinced, after
more than thirty years of study, not only that persistent existence
is a fact, but that occasional communication across the chasm—
with difficulty and under definite conditions—is possible. . . . The
evidence has thoroughly convinced me (1) of human survival, (2)
of the possibility under favourable circumstances, of communication
between the dead and the living, and (3) that death is only an
episode in a continuous existence. I also think it fairly established
that some kind of help, guidance or inspiration reaches us at times
across what is sometimes called "the gulf" or through what is often
called "the veil." . . . The hypothesis of continued existence in another set of conditions, and of possible communication across the
boundary, is not a gratuitous one made for the sake of comfort and
consolation, or because of a dislike to the idea of extinction; it is a
hypothesis which has been gradually forced upon the author—as
upon many other persons—by the stringent coercion of definite experience. The foundation of the atomic theory in chemistry is to
him no stronger. The evidence is cumulative, and has broken the
back of all legitimate and reasonable scepticism.[56]

Yet when apparent communication with the dead, offering the
most direct empirical evidence of the survival of the person, is
proffered, one of three attitudes, or a combination of them, is
quite customary. We can more usefully summarize these responses and weigh their worth by providing for the purpose of
analysis a composite illustration which includes principal features occurring in hundreds of cases appearing in the literature.

A few years ago in England an elderly vicar died, leaving his

[56] Quoted from Hart, *op. cit.* (n. 14, above), p. 11.

widow surviving. The clergyman had been a faithful, stable pastor to his congregation, but of somewhat Victorian bent in his personal relationships. In the family he had handled alone the financial matters, never discussing his decisions about such family matters as the disposition of his salary, although he always gave his wife an adequate allowance. At the time of his death his widow knew nothing of their monetary situation and searched vainly through his papers for some indication of savings accounts or other provision for her welfare. When she was unsuccessful in her search she sought help from the bishop of the diocese, believing herself to be penniless, since the Church of England did not provide a pension for widows of clergy. The bishop investigated and when his careful inquiries confirmed the findings of the widow, he secured some assistance for the aging woman.

While this was going on a priest from another part of England had been called to take charge of the parish. Neither he nor his family were acquainted with the former vicar or his wife. Shortly after they moved into the vicarage, the new priest, his wife, and children began to be disturbed by knockings and shuffling sounds which were confined to the study. At first the young couple assumed this was due to some natural phenomena of drafts and loose boards. The construction of the house was thoroughly checked, including the windows, chimneys, walls, floors, water pipes and heating conduits. Nothing out of order could be found. In checking the history of the structure they found that nothing similar had been noted before. Finally, feeling awkward, yet distracted and mystified by the continuing unexplained sounds, the new vicar took the matter up with the bishop.

After listening to the account, the bishop consulted with one of his clergy who was an expert in the field of psychic phenomena. Then he called a medium well known to the Church for her reliability, and with the widow all of them proceeded to the vicarage. In the living room the medium (who did not know the reason for her presence) in the company of the bishop, the advising priest, the vicar with his wife, and the widow attempted to establish contact with the deceased clergyman. Almost immediately the medium reported seeing the shadowy figure of a man, called him by name and described him accurately, and then seemed to engage in conversation with him. She then spoke to the widow and told her that her husband had died before he could tell her that he had hidden away securities and cash—a procedure which he thought to be the safest way to provide for their old age. Through the medium he then went on to express his unhappiness at realizing that he had failed to take his wife into his confidence and his frustration at not being "noticed" more quickly when he rustled papers, banged shutters, and produced the other sounds which had disturbed the present tenants. Then the medium described the exact location of the savings in the study adjoining the room in which they all sat. The bishop and the others together went and pried loose the panel described and behind it found precisely what was described by the medium. The medium expressed to the group the sense of peace now felt by the deceased and his assurance that no more disturbances would occur. The latter was quite correct, and the vicar thereafter reported no further unexplained sounds.

Earlier it was indicated that there were three, or a combination of three, possible attitudes usually taken by persons attempting to explain this, and similar, events. Purposely has been eliminated a fourth answer, which upon a little reflection will be seen to be no answer at all. Some people will simply regard all such happenings as fraud and the persons reporting and investigating them as falsifiers of one type or another. This is to make an assumption so vast and so unverifiable about so many people that it can be inferred that individuals subscribing to it are of the general psychological category as those who say "The earth is flat—my common sense tells me so."

But the first of those attempting to engage with the evidence realistically will be those who assume all the happenings to have explanations based in what is already known (and generally held to be true by their cultural peers) of the sciences of physics, geology, psychology, etc. Those of this persuasion then would analyze the foregoing illustration in a manner something like this:

The widow of the elderly vicar had unconsciously over the years been highly resentful of her husband's Victorian attitude which would have seemed to relegate her to an inferior position. She indeed knew of his hiding the securities and money, but repressed this knowledge along with her resentment of his treatment of her. At the time of the vicar's death she consciously believed herself to have been left without provision for her support. Also the bishop had been told by the elderly vicar of his hiding of the money but had, during the course of time, forgotten the conversation. Consequently when she applied for help both believed they were dealing with a real emergency. The young vicar, along with his family, certainly heard sounds but had not properly investigated the condition of the house or hadn't checked with the seismological department of the nearest university where earth tremors might have been recorded. Perhaps a sufficiently trained investigator might have discovered some meteorological disturbances centering on the exact location of the house—or more than likely the entire family "imagined" the sounds (with a kind of small-group auto-hypnosis having taken place).

When the bishop, in the presence of his adviser and the young vicar, called the medium on the telephone he indicated to her in some way unknown to, and undetected by, the men present (she being unusually perceptive) the nature of his business with her. She quickly, before the short time it took her to arrive by taxi, called a friend and obtained the names and descriptions of the dead vicar and his wife, believing this would facilitate the "sitting." While the widow was being driven to the diocesan office she, becoming suddenly unusually insightful, began to find the repression of the years diminishing and small bits of memory restored to her. When the sitting began, although the medium's eyes were ostensibly closed, actually she managed—in good faith but out of necessity—to blink occasionally (and—it having been noted that she was a woman of great perception) took in the fact that she was on the right track from the expressions on those faces of the assembled group that she was able to see during the rather protracted blink of her eyes.

Concurrently, the widow's repressed hostility toward her husband and repressed knowledge of the location of the money emerged to the surface. Immediately comprehending that she had in fact put the bishop to a good bit of trouble, the bereaved woman managed to signal the hiding place of the money to the medium who quickly and correctly figured which panel in the adjoining room the lady was pointing to. However, the medium, now being the one to repress in good faith the information so received during the longest yet of the eye blinks, reported to the group that she was finding the deceased vicar troubled. Perhaps the good bishop, also having forgotten that he really knew where the hoard was located, managed also to point to the spot (unconsciously) which was noted by the medium but by none of the others. She then told the group where to find the savings.

All satisfied, the episode ends, with but a few loose ends. The noises stopped. This, of course, is accounted for by the reversal of the conditions producing the sounds: the small earthquake, having as their epicenter the vicarage, are over, or the meteorological disturbances located in the region of the study are concluded, or—what is more likely, of course—the young vicar and his family are now released from the small-group post-auto-hypnotic suggestion originally induced by them. The careful scrutiny and acceptance of the entire event by responsible analysts (whose aim includes not only the chronicling of such events but the elimination of all that can be explained by any verifiable combination of causes other than communication with the dead) was also unconsciously motivated out of (a) respect for the bishop, the priest-adviser, and the widow, (b) conscious respect, but unconscious protective feelings for the good name of the medium. These motives caused the investigators unconsciously to repress any of the foregoing explanations for any one of the separate items. Finally, any items of the event not accounted for in this cause-effect manner are due to chance.

The second of the theories put forth as explicative is somewhat more sophisticated than the first, although it still relies heavily on armchair psychological explanations. It assumes the validity of most psychic phenomena, but puts forth the claim that communication with the dead is unbelievable and nonverifiable. This theory would relate to the phenomena in this way.

The reaction of the widow to her recently deceased husband and her repressed memory of the hiding of the money are the same as those just given. This, or the repressed memory of the bishop of the hiding of the money, is fairly essential to this version of the events. The others are relatively innocent of coincidental Freudian repressive malfunctionings. The knocking, shuffling sounds so disturbing to the new family are the result of psychokinesis and are emanating from the unconscious mind of either the widow or the bishop—who wish to be found out for obvious reasons. The new vicar's report of the disturbances stands and his attempts to detect physical reasons are genuine.

The meeting in the diocesan office is given this interpretation. When the phone call to the medium is made she, with absolute accuracy, detects the purpose (conscious or unconscious, or both) of his call by extrasensory perception. They all arrived at the office. After another deep level and surface level "reading" by telepathy takes place, the medium sizes up the entire situation. In this interpretation of the events, the medium is not only an unusually perceptive woman, she is also highly skilled in psychoanalytic techniques. The group gathers in the study. The medium now is gathering by telepathy from all the minds present the information pertinent about names and the physical description of the deceased. By precognition or clairvoyance she is able to determine the mental acceptance of her words by those who recognize the deceased man from her description of him. At this point some thought to the medium must be given, inasmuch as her innocence was postulated. One must assume that she now is hallucinating or is experiencing a psychic phenomenon known as clairaudience (the hearing of an internal voice), inasmuch as she states that she is speaking to a man. Here another psychic phenomenon must occur or we must assume that the medium is gathering the thoughts of a psychiatrist (whose existence was never imagined by any of those present) by telepathy. The new phenomenon consists of reading of "memory-traces"[57] of the deceased (incidentally, not recognized as a valid phenomenon by any consensus of those who have engaged in psychical research). This occurs when she expresses the unhappiness of the dead man caused by his not confiding in his wife. The finding of the money in the proper place can be assignable to the original assumption that either the widow or the bishop had a very poor memory but that the buried content of their minds was open to the telepathic psychoanalytic probing by the medium. The noises would stop when the widow's (and/or the bishop's) needs are filled. The sense of peace expressed by the medium is now obviously felt by everyone concerned and probably needs no explanation at all.

The first of these counter hypotheses suffers from many failures of omission and commission in logic and regard for the truth. One is struck almost immediately with not only the rather arrogant use, but with the almost awesome amount, of psychological information required to make the judgments concerning the deep-seated motivations of the persons involved in the experience. Most psychiatrists would make such evaluation only after lengthy and careful interviews with a patient; and other professional counselors would hesitate—using a more superficial working hypothesis as a basis for helping the counselee. Even at that, to assume that the psychological functioning of all the persons, from diverse backgrounds and of differing levels of education, would be in accord with their reported actions is an assumption so vast that it belongs in the category of faith rather than in that of "scientific" explanation.

To understand the actions of the vicar and his family on any basis given by those using this scientific/common sense rationale requires some more immodest faith leaps. The probability of an earthquake having as its epicenter the vicarage is extremely

57 Crookall, *op. cit.* (n. 14, above), p. 204.

slim. The small-group auto-hypnosis theory for the hearing of the noises by the family suffers from two difficulties: (a) the assumption that each member of the family would respond in the same way is doubtful, to say the least; and (b) the theory itself is not widely accepted among all psychiatrists, it still being thought of by some as a phenomenon of the same genre as that being refuted. The eye-blink sequences conjure up in the mind of most ordinarily reasonable people a scene produced and enacted by not too subtle professional comedians. The *concurrence* of all these events in itself would seem to require the greatest possible leap of sheer unsubstantiated faith, offending as it does that widely accepted guide used in logic, mathematics, and the other sciences of our day—Occam's Razor,[58] which in the social sciences is called the law of parsimony.[59] In paraphrase, the famous Razor warns against accepting a multiplicity of complex explanations until the simplest one has been absolutely proven wrong, then the simpler ones, and so on up the scale. This vital bit of medieval thinking helped clear the air for the coming Enlightenment, and to revert to earlier thinking must be seen as ridiculous for our "science/common sense" theorists.

The second composite of statements by those attempting to make the events easy to understand does not need quite so much analysis. An enumeration of the psychic events, with their varying degree of acceptance[60] is first in order:

[58] *Entia non sunt multiplicanda praeter necessitatem* ("Entities [of explanation] are not to be multiplied beyond need"), though commonly attributed to the fourteenth century William of Occam, actually originated with John Ponce of Cork in 1639, having been given the name "Occam's Razor" by Sir William Hamilton in 1852. W. M. Thorburn, "The Myth of Occam's Razor," *Mind*, XXVII (1927), pp. 345 ff., cited in Ducasse, *op. cit.* (n. 55, above).

[59] The source just cited indicates that the law of parsimony was formulated prior to Occam by Duns Scotus (Occam's mentor) and other philosophers of the period, using various forms of words; e.g., *Frustra fit per plura quod fieri potest per pauciora* ("The more is in vain when the less will serve [to account for the facts to be explained]").

[60] *A Speculation in Reality,* by Irving F. Laucks, Consultant, Center for the Study of Democratic Institutions (New York: Philosophical Library, 1953), pp. 126–27.

1. Telepathy
    (a) Of material being thought about by the subjects
    (b) Of material deeply repressed by the subjects
2. Precognition
3. Clairvoyance
4. Clairaudience
5. Psychokinesis
6. Memory-trace existence and recognition

Events accepted by some as "psychological" and by others as "psychic":

1. Autohypnosis and post-auto-hypnotic suggestion
    (a) Of one person
    (b) Of a small group
2. Hallucination

After accepting these several events one still needs to make the same detailed long-distance psychoanalytic evaluations, propose the diagnoses so indicated, and then accept as valid the working out of the various solutions to the problems of the assorted individuals and investigating groups. In the event the sophisticate is feeling a little intellectually feverish at this point, the assumption of an eye-blink here and there will probably not ameliorate his condition. The possibility of all these events being constellated about one certain deceased vicar almost defies even faith, unless the principle of synchronicity is invoked, although this would be a tautology—the term being descriptive and not explanatory. Occam's Razor can be handled in a variety of ways, no doubt ingenious, by those using this tortuous method of multiple, involved explanations—but it can never be acknowledged as plausible.

The third way of handling this group of events is the use of the formula: data + inference = modest faith-affirmation. The data outlined are generally accepted as the valid reportings of responsible and truthful persons. Neither judgmentalism nor secondhand psychoanalysis is utilized—both being considered emotional exercises not relevant under the circumstances to a sober consideration of the facts. We now have the event pretty much as described in the beginning. An inference is made—without regard to its emotional connotations to the observer, and in accordance with an established guide to correct thinking, Occam's Razor—that in this one case some kind of communication with the deceased vicar *was* established. Perceived by a number of persons simultaneously has been an assortment of data, but in and through the data and as its unifying reality (as in the case of relationship to any living person) has been the sensing of the *move* of a particular human personality. From our previous discussions of the psyche and the recorded observations of psychologists, anthropologists, physiologists, etc., we are ready to make a modest leap of faith. We are, by faith, ready to say that *personal survival of death is a fact, and that "what" survives is identifiable and unique, and represents a new phase in the existence of the person.*

Our jigsaw puzzle is now beginning to take on a cohesive shape and we are seeing that the missing pieces are fitting one or another of the several open places.

The implications of this are enormous and diversified, but need not result in an exclusivist position in theology, or even in psychology. The terror of death, the unbearable fears of having in childhood somehow lost a "gift" of eternal life through sin of one kind or another can be shed as the intolerable burdens they are. Ongoing life is seen as of the nature of the human being. It is *natural*, not "supernatural."

The Nature of Ongoing Life

Can more be affirmed than the mere fact of survival? Anyone raised in a culture in which Christianity, until these latter days, has been so prominent is accustomed to a much fuller picture than this. The Churches and their spokesmen (from pulpit and cathedral, in individual instruction and through the printed word) have proclaimed many, many certainties about "the next world." These propositions have been far from consistent with each other, either between different denominations or within the same denomination. But each of these many declarations has purportedly rested on one or another of the customary "infallible" bases of authority.

Without the employment of those bases, is there anything to say about life after death which can be legitimately inferred from observable data, adhering to the methodology we have sought to use up to this point? There is. But *fewer* things can legitimately be affirmed through the use of this more modest method.

The sources of relevant data are two: what we know about personhood as manifested in the here and now, and what appears to be the character of personhood hereafter, as it may be disclosed by reliable psychic phenomena. Any hypothesis supported by data from one of these two sources would of course be more convincing if it were at the same time supportable from the other. Since more evident to us is the functioning of persons in our present plane of existence, that is the best place to start.

The most characteristic feature of persons, as contrasted with things, is self-transcendence. This quality has at the heart of it *freedom of decision.* In modern times, in an era when political and economic developments have, in many parts of the world, diminished external limitations on personal freedom, we have at the same time, especially since Freud, become increasingly aware of internal limitations effected by familial and social conditioning and the past traumata of personal history. In fact progress in modern society has in many ways provided new matrices of conditioning and new causes of trauma. Nevertheless, for most individuals there is a certain measure of freedom, not only in response to the presentation of individual alternatives, occasion by occasion, but—more significantly for our present consideration—in response to profound encounters and confrontations. Persons can change in their basic outlook or their direction of living. Personal psychological development rarely proceeds in a uniform curve up or down a graph. Rather, in reaction to new and perhaps unexpected events, a person can "go free" of previous shackles and, with regard to that aspect of life, find himself on a new plateau. Or, in defensive response to precisely the same circumstances, he can tighten the shackles, and thereafter be less free in the given realm. Thus he will have shriveled rather than grown. This is the way it is with persons.

If there is ongoingness, what goes on is a person, not a thing. Therefore entailed in the affirmation of personal survival is freedom and the opportunity to grow and to shrink as a person.

So one thing becomes apparent: impossible is the conventional Christian doctrine that one's fate is settled as of the moment of death—a heaven of infinite bliss or a hell of infinite torment. Quite apart from any theological or moral considerations, such a finalized dichotomy contradicts plain facts about the nature and functioning of persons.

But the same conclusion is required from other considerations. The kind of persons who, under anybody's theology, would qualify for this heaven of infinite bliss would not be blissful there—knowing that elsewhere there were many have-nots, deprived, underprivileged. At the least, these blessed ones would stage a demonstration before the throne of the Most High. Should they achieve no results from that, they would certainly seek to organize a rescue party, a poverty program, or an Operation Headstart. Failing in any such moves, they would go to hell—to be alongside these others in their plight. Particularly would they if the Servant image of Jesus has been their model. In fact, that's where Jesus himself would be, if we can judge at all from what the New Testament tells us about his ministry. God would be all alone in his Heaven.

Moreover, the many instances of credible phenomena of communication with deceased persons reveal that they are finite human beings like ourselves, not oracles: there consistently appear to be limitations on their knowledge and notions. And in any number of cases there has been affirmation that change and growth is a potential in their scene. Not entirely convincing would be the mere expression of conviction about this (which could, by the legitimate application of the principle of Occam's

Razor or reductionism, be attributed to a view of the matter held by the medium or, at the most, by the deceased—who is no more infallible than any of us). However, in many cases of such communication there have been repeated instances where, in continued communication with the same person, the fact of his growth has been evidenced in the changes of attitudes, insights, and experiences revealed in the respective "sittings." Thus such communication, although far from telling us all about life to come, does give a plausible basis for inferring that ahead for all of us is the possibility of not only growing in knowledge and in capacity for awareness, but also in maturity as persons—possessing a greater capacity to love and be loved, to relate to others, and to serve them.

One way in which such ongoing development has been conceived is *reincarnation,* the view (held throughout history by people of various religious allegiances, or of none)[61] that spirits can be born again into earthly existence. Consistent with this doctrine is belief in a pre-existence of persons now living in this present time.

The belief is characteristic of Hinduism and Buddhism, the religions of ancient Egypt, and Zoroastrianism (still held today by the Parsees), and among the Sikhs, the Sufis, and the Druses. According to Josephus, this view was held by the Essene and Pharisee sects of the Jews, and it was also affirmed by Josephus himself and by Philo.

In light of the expectancy in later Judaism of the return of the prophet Elijah (Mal. 4:5), the New Testament conceives of John the Baptist as the reincarnated Elijah.[62] Reincarnation is implied in the Fourth Gospel and in the book of Revelation.[63]

Reincarnation was taught by Justin Martyr and Origen, and

---

[61] For a quite complete selection of writings from these various traditions and of Western thinkers in various countries, see *Reincarnation: An East-West Anthology,* edited by Joseph Head and S. L. Cranston (New York: Julian Press, 1961). See also Ducasse, *op. cit.* (n. 55, above), pp. 20–26. Cf. Jung, *op. cit.* (n. 14, above), pp. 316 ff.

[62] =Elias: Matt. 17:9–13; Mark 9:13; Matt. 11:11–15.

[63] John 9:34; Rev. 3:12.

also by two of the four men traditionally recognized as the "Greek Fathers," Clement of Alexandria and Gregory of Nyssa; and two of the "Latin Fathers," Jerome and Augustine, were open to the idea. Ever since, various Roman Catholic and Protestant thinkers have held this view. Also it was held in antiquity by Pythagorus and Plato and in modern times by Hume, Kant, Fichte, Schopenhauer, and Renouvier.

Many individuals have experienced what have seemed to be "flashbacks" to earlier existences, and in a number of such cases there seems to be some corroborating evidence.[64] But, just recently there have been published results of a study, using scientific methods, of a score of such cases in various countries, by Dr. Ian Stevenson, Professor in the Department of Neurosurgery, University of Virginia College of Medicine, and until recently chairman of that Department.[65] Whether or not reincarnation is the most plausible inference from the data (among those who accept such data as true, alternative hypotheses are proposed) would relate only to the *mode* of continued existence, not to the affirmation of either the reality of it or that personal life after death is one of development, involving individual freedom.

So what we know, from earthly experience, about the way personality develops (either in a constructive or a destructive direction) as well as what we can learn about the character of personhood through reliable psychic phenomena, plus the logic of the situation—all seem to indicate that the plausible expectation of the nature of personal life after death is that it will be of the same essential character (whatever the details of the environment) as personal life now. Such a conviction brings us right back to earth. It is here and now that we are called to learn, to work, to love and (hopefully) to be loved, to enjoy—and to grow. While, under such a conviction, we know that our time here is not all that there is for us, still there is in this view of things every motivation for moving to new plateaus of freedom and effectiveness, for becoming all we can become, while in

64 See works cited in notes 14, 15, and 51, above.
65 *Twenty Cases Suggestive of Reincarnation* (New York: American Society for Psychical Research, 1966).

these familiar surroundings. One world at a time.

If this is where our exploration has taken us, one might well ask, why have we bothered to ponder this matter of survival at all? There are at least two values in a plausibly grounded belief in the life to come. But one which has been stressed as such throughout Christian history is actually not a value, in fact quite the reverse: it can corrupt mature personal development.

What is referred to is the prospect of rewards and punishments in the next life used as a source of motivation for doing good and eschewing evil in this world. A prominent illustration is found in the Beatitudes and other parts of the Sermon on the Mount— much of which has been discovered in passages in the Dead Sea Scrolls. What by way of actions and attitudes is encouraged and discouraged is laudable. But the expressed basis of motivation is less than noble: rewards in heaven for well-doing, hellfire for evil-doing. Action or inaction on this basis may be prudence, but it is not virtue. Nor does it make for the best fulfillment of persons. It is a sign of real moral maturity when a person responds to a situation simply in terms of the claim of that situation. For example, he gives first priority to a significant need of another simply because that is where what he has to offer can then and there best be devoted. Conversely, he seeks to curb an impulse the acting out of which would seriously damage another—just because of that fact. In none of the examples, in the last chapter, of the "man for others" style of life does it appear that the motivation for the actions and words which showed forth truth-courage-love was hope for reward or fear of punishment—in this life or in the next.

Yet there are values in belief in personal conscious survival. They are not mentioned as *reasons* for the belief: if there is not a data-basis for affirming survival, it should not be affirmed, whatever psychological values might appear to arise from such a belief. But, since in fact there is, as we have seen from the outline of it at length, an empirical basis for this faith, it is appropriate—and fruitful—to recognize the positive values which flow therefrom.

Two which are discernible are the provision of direct answers to the basic and recurrent questions which our discussion at the beginning of this chapter brought to the fore. The first is the pressing one in time of bereavement. Is he dead for good? or does he live on? Will I see him again? Nothing—not memory of the deceased, not the fine example his life has provided for those who remain, not the sympathy (or even empathy) of friends—nothing can be as comforting and reassuring as a soundly based faith that all persons go on past death.

The second concern, quite apart from bereavement (though made more vivid at the time of another's death), is the pervasive fear of one's own death. As we saw, this fear is in the alternative: extinction/survival—but in hell. The fear in either form should be allayed by a reasonable belief in ongoing life with an open future.

CHAPTER VIII

GOD

"The decisive question for man," according to the late Dr. C. J. Jung, is, " 'Is he related to something infinite or not?' "[1]

This incisive statement points to the underlying affirmation that animates cultures of great diversity. Whatever particular religious or conceptual system may prevail, the root question "Is man related to something infinite or not?" recurs. Western man typically asks *Is there a God?* because he has been informed by the Judeo-Christian conceptuality. Oriental man asks *Is each the One?* and, asking his question in that fashion, gives expression to his Hindu-Buddhist metaphysical heritage. This same root question lies behind the here-and-now queries and mottoes of those in present day subcultures—whether existentialist, activist, or "dropout."

To take the more familiar of the examples (Is there a God?), it seems fair to say that the man who asks or answers such a question is not *decisively* interested in whether there is an additional being in the universe, however extraordinary such a being may be. His interest in such a question, to whatever degree, is of the same category as "Are there UFO's?" Rather, the real nature of his interest arises from a concern about his own person, its adequacy and its wholeness.

[1] *Memories, Dreams and Reflections*, p. 325.

"Am I"—in my finiteness and often fragmentary experiences and perceptions—"related" or relatable to—"something infinite?" —that is, reality that is not merely confining and partial? (And if so, how can I become less confined, less partial?)

For some persons, this question is really the decisive one. Many more will say that it is. But for many, the question is marginal in importance. Among these millions, many will readily enough affirm that there is a God, but His existence or nonexistence is actually low on the totem pole of their concerns.

This is why the late Paul Tillich, on the premise that to be religious is to be ultimately concerned, insisted that the serious atheist is more religious than many believers. He is ultimately concerned about the ultimate question; many a theist is not.

Hence, Dr. Jung's declaration is, descriptively, only partially true. Is it normatively true? Should all ask and seek the answer to the question he frames? The common response these days is not the proclamation of atheism (either in old style or in "historical" form—the "death of God"). The common response is the declaration—even by some theologians and clergy—that it really doesn't matter, one way or the other.

This outlook is not new; it has been the prevalent one, perhaps, all along. With most people, even churchgoers, less all-embracing and more concrete concerns take priority in making decisions. This focusing on "practical" matters to the exclusion of the more theological considerations marks Church leadership, whether its style be personal, priestly, or politically ambitious. Whatever the pious rationalization, a shunning of ultimate questions may be all too evident.[2]

What is different about the diffidence about God today is its frank articulation. This frankness is not simply on the part of persons seeking to be free of the moral claims customarily connected with "the fear of God," but on the part of many who are deeply committed to responsible living, dedicated to the "man for others" model, exalting (and displaying) truth-courage-love.

[2] A wealth of convenient and "acceptable" rationalizations are provided in Charles Merrill Smith's How to Become a Bishop Without Being Religious (Garden City, N.Y.: Doubleday, 1965).

Many like Jim Reeb, who in going to Selma risked laceration by bull-whip, maiming by horses' hoofs, and wounding from the bullets of official and unofficial gun-wielders, would have joined him in saying the God-question doesn't matter. On hand too were God-is-dead spokesmen as part of the effort to extend to Negroes the chance for *man* to be fully alive. Paradoxically, few, if any, in the local subculture—including those of the gendarmerie, equipped with the bull-whips, the horses, and the guns, would have breathed the thought (or have let themselves consciously believe) that whether there is a God doesn't matter— let alone that He's dead or that He never was.

So the all-too-common assignment, to those who have rejected any idea of a living God or are diffident about it, of the motive of antinomianism—that they want to be free of morality and "live it up"—is not only judgmental (hence in itself unethical[3]), it is unverifiable. Or, to stay more closely to the method which informs the analysis in this book, available data do not support a generic inference which could form the basis of such a judgment. In fact the data we have,[4] not the least the correlation of orthodoxy and ethics suggested by the attitude and behavior of the locals in the illustration used, would—on the surface at least—support quite the opposite inference.

For the more thoughtful of the "it doesn't really matter" school the diffidence about God is far from casual. In fact some of the reasoned support for it matches up with a conclusion reached in the last chapter. Few of the *diffidentes* about whom we have been talking would affirm life after death; but though in the preceding pages this belief is affirmed on the basis of data + faith, it is also insisted that, whether or not there is life ahead, it shouldn't figure in the motivation for how one lives here and now.[5] So, in that connection, it really doesn't matter.

Now if the supposed eternal sanctions customarily linked with God don't matter, does He matter?

Yes. The data on the very question of the relation of an un-

3 See *You and the New Morality: 74 Cases*, Chap. 13.
4 See pp. 22–23 and note 36, p. 70, above.
5 See p. 161, above.

folding, fulfilling, serving style of life to belief in God show that it *does* matter. The God-believers are shown to be more unethical in direct proportion to their orthodoxy.[6] But an obvious explanation comes to mind: It is not that the firmness of belief in God is the *cause* of closed, judgmental, hating personality deformity. Rather, persons like that are the ones more likely to believe in God, more likely to cling to the supports belief in God represents. This is more starkly evident at the extreme end of the spectrum in orthodoxy: here we have a high proportion of insecure, exclusivist, xenophobic, in-group types who are internally frightened about the removal, or even the shifting, of any of their small props. These are the ones whose characteristic view of God is displayed as they sing in plaintive tones,

> I need thee, O, I need thee
> Every hour I need thee . . .[7]

and

> Rock of ages, cleft for me
> Let me hide myself in thee; . . .[8]

and hymns and prayers about bulwarks and fortresses. Dr. Alan Watts says that man needs these less than learning to float and swim.[9] But these people can't float and swim (though in the subculture into which many of them have climbed, the home swimming pool is one of the status symbols: for a while it looked as though the home air raid shelter would achieve the same popularity—it would have been a better symbol of the mentality). Church attendance and literal Biblical orthodoxy is highest among those who have genericized into a "Communist plot" the objects of all their anti's—the U.N., the N.C.C., racial integration, mental health, fluoridation, "pornography," etc., etc., and who, when grouped in communities or clubs (sometimes ecclesiastical ones) of similar types, nourish in each other a mass

---

6 See n. 4, above.
7 *The* [Episcopal] *Hymnal 1940*, Hymn 438.
8 *Ibid.*, Hymn 471.
9 *Beyond Theology* (New York: Pantheon, 1964), pp. 113–15.

paranoia. Fearful of being other than simplistic, they have black-and-white answers for everything; any grays are threatening to them as persons. This is not overstated about members of the religious "radical right"; there are many more to be found a few inches to the left of the right, for whom it is true in lesser degree—but true.

However, does this not argue that their sturdy belief in God is an effect, not a cause? Yes and no. They and the likes of them in past eras (especially when before the dawn of the scientific era and the abolition or vitiation of droves of genuine bases of fear, there was a far higher percentage of them) formed a concept of God which projected on a cosmic screen their ignorance and dread of the unknown, their hatred of the nonconformist. The result has been an effect of terrestrial sickness. But in turn it has been an antidote to its cure—and is a cause of sickness in millions who might not otherwise have contracted it. "They become like what they behold," to use William Blake's well-known words.

The God thus projected by subjects and becoming then a subject is also "the God in the gaps."[10] Not merely providing a mental semantic for unknown causality, He has actually resisted his own dimunition. He has provided a substitute for real answers and has deadened the instinctive quest to find them; He was on the side of the restriction or annihilation of those trying to find out or seeking to communicate what had been found out.[11] As Sir Julian Huxley has said, "The God hypothesis is no longer of any pragmatic value for the interpretation or comprehension of nature, and indeed often stands in the way of

[10] See Bishop John A. T. Robinson, *A New Reformation?* (Philadelphia: Westminster Press, 1965), Appendix I, pp. 106 ff., reprint of his address at the Exhibition on Atheism, University of Frankfurt, entitled "Can a Truly Contemporary Person *Not* Be an Atheist?" (to which his answer is finally "yes," after recognizing the validity of such critiques as those cited in the notes below).

[11] He is the God of the Tennessee legislators who voted to keep on the books the anti-evolution law publicized in 1926 through the "monkey trial," *The New York Times*, April 21, 1967, p. 5. (But under threat of litigation initiated in the name of a teacher, they thereafter repealed the act.)

better and truer interpretations."[12] True words from an atheist—
and the same from a devout Lutheran pastor: but more—he
embraces the field of ethics as well as that of science. Dietrich
Bonhoeffer wrote while in a Nazi prison:

> Man has learned to cope with all questions of importance without
> recourse to God as a working hypothesis. In questions concerning
> science, art, and even ethics, this has become an understood thing
> which one scarcely dares to tilt at any more. But for the last hundred
> years or so it has become increasingly true of religious questions also;
> it is becoming evident that everything gets along without "God," and
> just as well as before. As in the scientific field, so in human affairs
> generally, what we call "God" is being more and more edged out of
> life, losing more and more ground. . . .[13]

Then he goes further, projecting beyond the present churchly
defenses:

> Christian apologetic has taken the most varying forms of opposi-
> tion to this self-assurance. Efforts are made to prove to a world thus
> come of age that it cannot live without the tutelage of "God." Even
> though there has been a surrender on all secular problems, there
> still remain the so-called ultimate questions—death, guilt—on which
> only "God" can furnish an answer, and which are the reason why
> God and the Church and the pastor are needed. . . . But what if
> one day they no longer exist as such, if they too can be answered
> without "God"?[14]

Actually it is not clear that for one of "the so-called ultimate
questions," death, "only 'God' can furnish an answer . . ." The
reader may not have noticed it, but in the preceding chapter on
life after death God was not mentioned; nor did any act or decision of His—nor even His existence—form any part of the
analysis. Considered was a variety of data relating to ψ in man
tending to confirm that in the here and now he transcends
both space and time limits and to the phenomena for which the
most plausible explanation appears to be communication with

---

[12] *Religion Without Revelation* (London: Max Parrish, 1957, second
edition), p. 58.
[13] *Letters and Papers from Prison* (New York: Macmillan, 1958), p. 145.
[14] *Ibid.*, p. 146.

the dead—from which was inferred, and affirmed by faith, that the conscious personality goes on past the grave. Declared was no dogma that God raises up the dead (or selected ones of their company). A quite democratic view was presented: it is for all men, and because of the nature of what man is.

One of the arguments customarily used for life after death (and also as a partial answer to the age-old problem of evil) is that the obvious injustices and inequities men enjoy or suffer in this life can be put to rights in another one. But there is no empirical basis for this argument. It assumes more knowledge as to the nature and ways of God than we know or have any way of finding out. Similarly it assumes more knowledge of the arrangements after death than we have any factual or inferable way of knowing.

The consideration is not an irrelevant one: it falls in the same category as the comfort that belief in survival affords in bereavement and the answer it provides to the fear of death. As we saw, *if* one believes in ongoing life, these values indubitably exist; but the fact that the belief has these values neither proves it nor adds data to that from which the affirmation can plausibly be made. When it is used as an attempt at proof, it deserves the unbeliever's retort, "Wishful thinking!" So with the argument that if God is, He would raise all or some from the dead in order to even all scores. Within the terms of the data + faith method, personal survival as natural—not supernatural—has been affirmed and it would have been whether or not, using the same method, belief in God—which we are now considering—can be affirmed. Yet a yes to survival speaks to the problem of evil.

The other example Bonhoeffer gives—guilt, and its cognate, divine forgiveness—can for the moment signify a whole area in which the negative of man's need and the positive of matching experience seeming to meet the need, could point the existence of God as under one of the alternate hypotheses to be discussed. And this regardless of the rapid rate at which the increase of scientific knowledge is pushing "the God in the gaps" to the perimeter of reality. Apart from this one realm, which we will examine in due time, there is no basis through the method to which we are committed for arguing with any of the three trenchant sentences with which Bishop John Robinson summarizes the "three motives which have impelled men, particularly over the past hundred years, to question the God of their upbringing and ours":[15]

1. God is intellectually superfluous.
2. God is emotionally dispensable.
3. God is morally intolerable.

The case for these three declarations has been made adequately elsewhere;[16] here only enough will be said to indicate that grounds for belief in God cannot be found in these quarters, before taking a serious look at a category of data from which possibly a faith-affirmation reasonably can be made.

  1. There have been thought to be two reasons, intellectually, for positing God as the missing x to complete the picture: to fill in, in the case of the unexplainable, and to provide the first cause of all reality. A useful example of the first category is provided by a comparison of the astronomical analyses of Newton and Laplace.[17] The mathematics of the former could not account for certain clearly observable irregularities in the functioning of the solar system; so he credited them to God's direct intervention. But the mathematical problems were solved a little more than a century later by Laplace, who then came up with the over-all generalization that the planetary system is stable and that rather than vitiating the general equilibrium, what Newton had thought were irregularities were in fact essential to this equilibrium. Thereafter he is reported to have said of God to Napoleon, "I have no need of that hypothesis." His comment, as Dean Alan

15 *Op. cit.*, p. 107.
16 *Ibid.*, pp. 107–14; Alan Richardson, "The Death-of-God Theology," *Religion in Life*, Vol. 36, No. 1 (Spring, 1967), pp. 70 ff., at 73–74; Bertrand Russell, *Why I Am Not a Christian* (New York: Simon & Schuster, 1957); Michael Novak, *Belief and Unbelief* (New York: Macmillan, 1965), especially pp. 9–24; Barbara Wootton, *Testament for Social Science* (London: Unwin, 1950).
17 See Richardson, *op. cit.*, p. 73.

Richardson points out, "proves not that he was an atheist but that he was a better theologian than Newton."

On the other hand, to establish God as the "First Cause" is tautological. Thus to explain the type of reality we know is simply to recognize the mystery and either to raise the question, Who made God? (or, How did He get started?) or to invite the imagination to grasp what our finite minds cannot encompass, the concept of "always was."[18] As long as the inconceivable has to be inferred, namely, that there must always have been s(S?)omething, it could be declared to be a single particle (or, more likely, two particles, making possible interaction—hence development), or God, or a prior being who created God—or b(B?)eings in an infinite regression.

2. Belief in gods or a God has long served as a prop to man's sense of security. That this was true not only under primitive and superstititious religions is revealed by platitudes still in use in many quarters, such as "Don't worry; God will provide," "You can always count on God; He won't let you down." For many who would report to a Gallup pollster that they believe in God, actual involvement with Him is limited to emergencies, as is illustrated by an affirmation (doubtless with an empirical base) which originated during the last war and which was fairly impressive on first hearing: "There are no atheists in foxholes." The author remembers vividly an emergency trip in a single engine two-passenger plane whose pilot had declared early in the flight to his Episcopal priest-passenger that he had been raised a Roman Catholic but didn't believe in anything any more. Yet in landing, in immediate succession to a small craft which

[18] We can encompass eternity in the other direction, i.e., the future, simply by the negative process of not conceiving of an end of things; but no such device is available in the opposite direction. This distinction is reflected in the age-old and constantly used (at least five times in the service of Matins in our Anglican Churches) conclusion of the *Gloria Patri: "sicut in principio et nunc et semper, per omnia saecula saeculorum."* The "always" is an open-ended word and its open-endedness is further emphasized by the addition of "world without end" (literally, "throughout all ages of ages"), whereas "in the beginning" is not only inadequate to express eternity backwards, it is actually a contradiction of the concept.

had cracked up, the pilot hastily made the sign of the cross as he dipped toward the field.

There are two difficulties with this basis for belief in God. First, that He actually "comes through" in times of need—however properly and insistently implored—is far from verifiable; in fact there is a good deal of contrary experience. Second, required is belief in the doctrine of Special Providence. As the author has shown elsewhere,[19] it is unduly anthropomorphic to regard God as making particular decisions in this way. He does not tinker; He plays no favorites. He is "without variableness, neither shadow of turning" (Jas. 1:17, A.V.). As Bishop Robinson has said:

. . . There are some forms of belief in providence which merely pander to emotional immaturity. And these are the forms which secretly retain God in the gaps of our ignorance or fears, or which see Him as a celestial manipulator rearranging, interrupting, or taking over from, the forces which would otherwise be at work. And when these forces are those of human responsibility their "providential overruling" can quickly lead to the debilitation, the superstition and even the fatalism, of which the atheists accuse the religious.[20]

No atheists in foxholes? When the phrase was a "hit," no statistical surveys were produced as to the belief patterns of men whose military service required them to frequent foxholes. But directly entailed in the statement are two convictions: that men with such stark reasons for fear and terror would for that reason believe in God, and that belief in God would quiet their fear because He would protect those who believed in Him.[21] Attributed to Jesus is the observation that the rain rains on the just and the unjust alike (Matt. 5:45); and this is just as true of a rain of machine gun bullets as it is of an aqueous downpour. We were told of the infantryman (American, of course) preserved because a pocket Testament in his shirt pocket blunted the force of

---

[19] *A Time for Christian Candor*, Chap. 7 ("God and the Particular").

[20] *Essay in the New Christianity*, edited with introduction by William R. Miller (New York: Dell, 1967), p. 125.

[21] Perhaps an alternative conviction was implied: fear of death and trust in God for entry into heaven; regarding this see pp. 114 ff., above.

a bullet. Would the presence in the same pocket of a small pornographic paperback of equal thickness have failed to effect this result? If fear + naïve trust of this type is the basis of theism, there *should* have been atheists in foxholes!

3. The first two grounds for atheism outlined (God intellectually superfluous, emotionally dispensable) are "cool" rejections; the third is—and always has been—a bitter one, felt as well as thought: God is morally intolerable. And it is one which is constantly gaining strength in a world where everything is becoming magnified, evil no less than good, and in a culture which, whatever its moral faults, has seen an ever increasing sensitivity to evil. As to the first, one need only be reminded that the United States has dropped more bombs on little North Vietnam than we dropped on powerful Germany in World War II. Napalm wasn't invented then, and nuclear weapons of present-day magnitude did not exist when the United States dropped the only one ever visited on a city. As to the second, we need only recall the indifference to child labor and white supremacy—to take but two of many, many possible examples, in more "God-fearing" days.

When people say today that there is a decline in morals they are generally referring to what has indubitably been a freer attitude toward pre- and extra-marital sex, what is presumed to be an increase in homosexual acts (and as to this what may be involved is simply a greater knowledge of, and freer public discussion of, this form of activity), and what statistically is shown to be an increase in the incidence of crime. Generally overlooked in the sweeping generalization is the ever heightening sensitivity on the part of more and more people about social evils which denigrate persons and deny equal opportunity or any opportunity at all; a much more articulate protest against public-sponsored killings, for example, through capital punishment,[22] and the present non-war in Vietnam; and more concern about pain and

[22] For example, there has been a marked decrease in references to retribution as a support for the practice: (cf. "Vengeance is mind, I will repay, saith the Lord" [Rom. 12:19]). And there is increasing recognition

distress to millions throughout the world caused by hunger, disease, and inordinate population growth.[23]

When there was a higher percentage of persons believing in a personal God than there is now, there was much less concern about such moral problems. There is not necessarily a correlation between the two facts; but the existence of them certainly modifies declarations, still very common today, of a positive correlation of a belief in God and the soundness of morals. The point here is that today the long-standing block to belief in God because of evil in the world (an age-old problem having long earned its own categorization as a branch of theology under the now less frequently used term Theodicy) has been gaining increasing force and is expressed by a higher proportion of the population and with more intensity by many, many sensitive persons not much accustomed to engaging in metaphysical thought or argument. It is with this point alone that God is tersely dismissed and along with it there is often a "put-down"—with overtones of feeling—of the Church. Bishop Robinson cites as an example the impromptu words of a nineteen-year-old girl interviewed by the London *Daily Mirror* (and she might as well have been from Walla Walla or Keokuk—one hears words of similar effect everywhere):

"Do you believe in God?"
"No. I used to, but not now. I don't see how there can be a benevolent God. There are too many tragedies—personal and in the world. . . . RELIGION IS DISGUSTING."[24]

The Church itself set things up for a fall on this point, not by its affirming of belief in God, but by its universal insistence that He is omnipotent, omniscient, and omnibenevolent, leaving

of the fact that capital punishment is not a deterrent to crime, as is shown clearly by the American Law Institute report, the British Royal Commission report, and the Canadian Royal Commission report. See also: Gerald Gottlieb, *Capital Punishment* (Santa Barbara: Center for the Study of Democratic Institutions, 1966).

23 The magnificent encyclical of Pope Paul, *Progressio Populorum* (March 28, 1967), while obviously a stimulus to greater effort is also a symbol of the widespread concern which has been developing over the years.

24 "For These Girls It Is All Happining," March 5, 1964 (by-line story by Marjorie Proops, reporter).

no "out" for laying the blame for evil right on His shoulders. To
put it bluntly, If He's all that strong, all that smart, and all that
nice, why are so many things such a mess? Sometimes a lame
attempt was made to absolve Him of the responsibility by a
twin assertion that He does the good things while the bad things
are done by the Devil; but this doesn't help since this Devil is
His creation. Under some ways of putting it[25] he has directed
Satan to do the evil; under other analyses, though being all
powerful, he reluctantly lets the Devil (conceived of as a fallen
angel) have his way.[26]

But equally common has been the crediting of specific evils
directly to God. In the Church of England's *Book of Common
Prayer,* the priest is instructed to say to the patient, "Whatever
your sickness is know certainly that it is God's visitation." This
is certainly unqualified and right to the point! The American
Episcopal Prayer Book puts it more piously by clothing this
teaching in prayer form:

Almighty, everliving God, Maker of mankind, who does correct
those whom thou dost love, and chastise every one whom thou dost
receive; We beseech thee to have mercy upon this thy servant visited
with thine hand, and to grant that he may take his sickness patiently
. . . [followed by a reference to His "gracious will"][27]

However, there has been a movement away from such talk,[28]
not to other explanations which would be viable,[29] but to fuzzy
phrases or to calls to action—personal or corporate—against
specific evils or invitation to religious experience which will

25 The obvious example is the book of Job.

26 E.g., Rev. 12:7–12.

27 P. 321.

28 E.g., it is suspected that most Episcopal priests in celebrating the
Eucharist in a sickroom use the alternative Collect afforded by the 1928
revision of the Prayer Book (though the form quoted above was not voted
out by the General Convention—and was left in first place [p. 321 *vs.* p.
322]: a concept of God which for many is "morally intolerable" is apparently gratifying to others and does something for them; in any case, it
doubtless does something *to* them; cf. Blake's "They become like what they
behold."

29 There are none. See the summary and the analyses of eight of them
in *A Time for Christian Candor,* Chap. 6 ("Good out of Evil").

enable sufferers better to endure evil or to seek to create good out of it.[30]

Yet increasing quiet on the part of spokesmen of the Church about the causation of evil by God has by no means reduced the force of this inference as the principal cause of both popular and sophisticated atheism. The combination of orthodox teaching, as summed up in the creedal affirmation *one God the Father Almighty, Maker of heaven and earth, And of all things visible and invisible*, and of the easily observable fact of evil—of non-human origin as well as of human origin—logically leads to only one conclusion. As John Robinson has summed it up, it "reverses Voltaire's dictum that 'if God did not exist, we should have to invent Him.' It says rather: 'If God did exist, we should have to abolish Him!' "

This widespread feeling is an illustration of the fact that "wishful thinking" can work both ways. There is a good deal of it behind the current interest in the *necrotheologians*—those proclaiming the death of God.[31] Regardless of the logic of the situa-

[30] *Ibid.*, pp. 87–91.

[31] For example: Thomas Altizer and William Hamilton, *Radical Theology and the Death of God* (Indianapolis: Bobbs-Merrill, 1966); Altizer, *The Gospel of Christian Atheism* (Philadelphia: Westminster Press, 1966); Altizer, *Mircea Eliade and the Dialectic of the Sacred* (Philadelphia: Westminster Press, 1963); Hamilton, *The New Essence of Christianity* (New York: Association Press, 1961); Hamilton, "The Death of God," *Playboy*, August, 1966, pp. 79 ff. (cf. a critique by the present author and reply by Dr. Hamilton in *Playboy*, November, 1966, pp. 10–14).

Cf. Paul Van Buren's *The Secular Meaning of the Gospel* (New York: Macmillan, 1963); on the basis of modern semantic analysis the author takes the position that the God concept can have no objective referent—in short, it doesn't mean anything. More recently Dr. Van Buren has indicated that he places theology in the humanistic studies and that his concern with religion is as a human and cultural phenomenon. "Theology in the Context of Culture," in the *Christian Century's* series "How I Am Making Up My Mind," Vol. 82 (1965), pp. 428–30.

For analyses of the thinkers of this school see Thomas W. Ogletree, *The Death of God Controversy* (Nashville: Abingdon Press, 1966), and the symposium in *Religion and Life*, Vol. 36, Spring, 1967; for a comparison of "right wing" and "left wing" radicals see the article in this symposium by Lonnie D. Keiever, "Mapping the Radical Theologies," pp. 8–27. For a bibliography see J. A. Sanders' compilation in *Union Seminary Quarterly Review*, Vol. 21 (1966), pp. 182–84.

tion, there are many who would like to have it so. While some
display a mood of sadness and nostalgia in their announcement
of His demise, others stress not only that it should be accepted—
men should positively will it. There is a valid basis for both of
these moods with regard to the picture of God which has been
conventionally presented.

It is a normal part of the maturing of any individual that he
feels a sense of pain at the loss of childhood securities and that
at the same time he resents arbitrary authority hovering over
him. No matter what kind of parents he has, a youth emerging
into manhood both fears and desires his freedom. This familiar
experience in the life of each of us is being replicated in the
human situation as a whole in a time described by some as "man
come of age." This characterization is scorned by orthodox
spokesmen. There is basis for their scorn if it is taken to mean
that people are now conspicuously showing themselves capable
of running life and affairs well; there is too much obvious evidence to the contrary. But the description is true in the important
sense. What we in fact do and how well we do it is one thing;
where the responsibility lies for decision and action is another.

With more and more people—of all age levels—the old authority bases are gone, and the capacity of man to learn about
the functioning of reality and to shape his destiny is now well
established. There is no turning back. There is no way that the
"God" whom we could alternately lean on and blame can be made
credible again. With the triumph of the empirical method, and
with the emergence of a free society allowing open articulation
of the logic exposing the contradictions inherent in the old God-
concept, this God is dead. The cosmic projection of our ignorance
and fears is no more. To the degree that talk of the death of God
has served as a focus for greater awareness that this is the case,
such talk has served nobly the purposes of honesty, liberation,
and human responsibility.

However, some proponents of what is styled "radical theology"
insist that they are saying more. For them it is not only that,
descriptively, God figures less with man today, not only that the

old concept is no longer possible for man. They are affirming that a transcendent God who actually did exist has—as an historical event—actually died in our history. The other meanings of the proclamation are undeniably true; but how tenable is this stark historico-ontological doctrine?

On the historical side, necrotheologians are not uniform as to precisely when this death occurred. For example, like all Gaul it is divided into three parts: for Dr. Hamilton the Incarnation was "the beginning of the death of God"; "the nineteenth century lived that reality and instructs us to do the same" and "just now . . . it is our turn to understand and accept."[32] Dr. Altizer is more explicit: God totally poured Himself into Christ and the death of Jesus on Calvary (sans Resurrection) = the death of God; and the power of the living Word was thus released into a new and liberated humanity.

As an *historical* affirmation, it is one not only in fact lacking in any basis in verifiable data, it is one for which—because of the Subject-matter of the affirmation—no data would—or will —be available.

As an *ontological* affirmation, it is subject to two difficulties. First, the less anthropomorphic and capricious the concept of God, the more plausible would appear this simple logic: if He was, He is; if He isn't, He wasn't. But more later about a viable concept of God and the bases of affirming that He was/is or that He isn't/wasn't. But to theist and atheist alike should be evident the pre-Copernican character of the assertion that God died as an event "in our history." We have known for some time now that our earth is only one of many planets rotating around a small star in one galaxy of a vast universe. And on this planet, if we would arrange human history on a twelve-month calendar, the time the birth of Jesus is reported would come about noon on New Year's Eve. To say that an Event or events in this miniscule portion of the human history of our little planet could mark the end of Whoever or whatever is ultimate in the universe is an exaggerated form of geocentric parochialism.

32 *Playboy*, August, 1966, *loc. cit.*

But as we shall see, there is a sense in which history has something to do with what we may be able to say about God, if He is at all.

Is He? We can start from one of two directions. If we start with the conventional concept of God we must pare Him down every time we learn more about the workings of the natural order. In this case He keeps dying "by inches"—"the death by a thousand qualifications" as Professor Anthony Flew has put it.[33] The last gasp of this evermore weakened deity is just a matter of time.

But instead of starting from the top down (the supernatural superstructure for thought, which is collapsing) we can start from the bottom up—the real world. Does this real world provide any basis for inferring that there is any more than what its own observed (and, theoretically, observable) components add up to? To sharpen the question: Much has been observed; not as much —but much—has been understood; and these linked processes are advancing at an astonishing rate of speed. In principle there is no limit: in theory all the components will be surveyed and all will be understood. But assume that that has occurred. Will all that there *is* then be understood?

The suspicion that the answer is Yes has been growing since the spurt in machine building from the eighteenth century on. As a start it was easy to analogize contraptions and the people who made them. "What is heart but a spring," Hobbes wrote, "and the nerves but so many strings and the joints but so many wheels, giving motion to the whole body?"[34] Inevitable has been the expansion of this outlook: "tinkering about in their shops . . . men would see the world as a huge machine subdivided into an infinite number of lesser machines."[35]

But this does not say all. A machine does not reflect on its own being. It was early in the days of cybernetics that the French

[33] *New Essays in Philosophical Theology*, edited by Anthony G. N. Flew and Alistair C. MacIntyre (New York: Macmillan, 1955), pp. 96–97.
[34] Quoted in Loren Eiseley, *The Immense Journey* (New York: Vintage, Random House, 1946), p. 181.
[35] *Ibid.*

scientist, Lecomte du Noüy, while asserting that there is virtually no limit to what computers would be able to do, singled out one question such a machine could never answer, one question, namely, "Why a computer?"[36] Dr. Eiseley thus speaks of man's emergence in the evolutionary story ("once he had 'crossed over' into this new invisible environment"):

> He was becoming something the world had never seen before—a dream animal—living at least partially within a secret universe of his own creation and sharing that secret universe in his head with other, similar heads. Symbolic communication had begun. Man had escaped out of the eternal present of the animal world into a knowledge of past and future. . . . The Eden of the eternal present that the animal world had known for ages was shattered at last. Through the human mind time and darkness, good and evil, would enter and possess the world.[37]

What is here described historically is something experienced every day. Assume that a particular person is subjected to every mode of investigation—*totally* (projecting the future of the physical, psychological, and behavioral sciences). Yet there is *more* and will always be more: unique transcendent personhood.[38] It is this *more* which may be directly intuited, confronted, and engaged with, by another of the human species. Some of the facets of this *more* were spelled out earlier.[39]

A person is not only talked about; he is addressed as a *Thou* and addressed as such by an *I*. He is an object, but not only an object—he is a subject. This is evident too from our earlier analysis of the various categories of data for which the symbol ψ is used. The latter provided an adequate basis for affirming the extension of the unified person beyond the components, however fully surveyable, which are confined to space and time.

Another form of expressing the transcendent element is given

[36] *Human Destiny* (New York: David McKay Co., 1947), p. 125.
[37] *Op. cit.*, pp. 120–21.
[38] Cf. W. Stern's *"Unitas multiplex"* concept of the defining characteristic of a person, utilized by Professor Edgar S. Brightman in *Personality and Religion* (New York: Ronald Press, 1958), p. 35.
[39] See pp. 92 ff., and 118 ff., above.

us by the French Marxist, Roger Giraudy. With reference to the
innate capacity of man to transcend the given here-and-now
situation, he says:

If we are Communists . . . we perfectly understand the need,
brought forth by suffering, for perfect communion and for a love so
all-embracing that those who suffered never believed they could find
it anywhere but in God. Indeed, we find it a beautiful thing that
man, in his suffering, conceived such dreams, such hopes, conceived
the infinite love of Christ. It is this act of faith that proves that man
never considers himself wholly defeated. And thus he witnesses to
his greatness. This is why we neither despise nor criticize the Christian for his faith, his love, his dreams, his hopes. Our own task is
to labor and to struggle, lest they remain eternally distant or illusory.
Our task as Communists is to draw near to man in his most glorious
dreams and his most sublime hopes, to draw near to him in a real
and practical way, so that Christians themselves might find here on
our earth a beginning of their heaven.

. . . . .

It is true that we cannot take a step in the domain of thought or
action without affirming, by our act itself, the possibility and necessity of an order. At the root of every scientific hypothesis which seeks
to realize a new unification of appearances, there is the postulate
of the certain existence, outside of us and independently of us, of
a rational order. My *project* is to reflect it. At the root of every
political or moral enterprise which seeks to realize a higher form of
unification of the world—such as the classless society of Communism
will be—there is the postulate that history has a meaning and that
the realization of the total man is a realizable project. The philosophy
of the absurd is neither for the learned man nor for the revolutionary.
Neither is it for the believer.[40]

"No man has ever seen God" (1 John 4:12). The unknown
author of these words makes the connection between man and
God when he says ". . . he who does not love his brother whom
he has seen, cannot love God whom he has not seen" (1 John
4:20b). The same connection can be made, not only in terms of
the love relationship but in terms of affirmation of the ultimate
Reality. The whole scientific enterprise has focused on learning

[40] *From Anathema to Dialogue* (London: Herder & Herder, 1966), pp.
86, 110.

more and more about the respective components in the observable world—"that which we have seen" and, a priori, we assume that to the degree we haven't seen, given time, we will see. The scientific enterprise is dedicated to discerning the interconnections between, and the dynamic relationships of, the respective items and categories of reality. In this confident task, a basic premise and an operative assumption—one which is pragmatically successful—is that *there is a universe*. To put it plainly, it all hangs together.

Now, just as in the case of a narrower subject to which many particular sciences contribute investigation and understanding, namely, man, the total is greater than the sum of the parts, it is reasonable to affirm the same of the universe; there is a *Unus* in the universe. In and with, "under" and "beyond" all the particulars is a unifying, constellating Reality. In adopting this etymological device as a mode of expression, the choice of a personal ending for the adjective used as a noun (that is, the use of *Unus*[41] rather than *unum*) is quite deliberate. *Unum* might be adequate if personality, human transcendence, had not evolved in the universe. (But had it not there would be no one around able to use the word, or any words, or any concepts that lie behind words—concept-making and word-making being possible only through human transcendence.) The fact is that that which we express through inadequate words like "transcendence," "personality," "person," "the more"[42] has evolved. So any affirmation, or word or phrase to express the unifying Base of all reality, logically cannot ignore the plain fact of the personal which exists as part of what makes up the universe as we know it. The use of an impersonal word would not only ignore this evident aspect of reality, it would explicitly exclude it.

Though no scientist would make any claims to accuracy in dating the beginning of the evolutionary process or of the emer-

---

[41] *Una* might well be as appropriate. In spite of the acculturated bias in favor of a masculine image for God there is no verifiable basis for affirming either masculinity or femininity!

[42] See references in n. 39, above.

gence of man,[43] a fairly good working estimate of when things began is about 5,000,000,000 B.C. The first homonid (that is, manlike creature), *Australopithecus,* appeared on the scene about 1,000,000 B.C. and *Homo sapiens* (Cro-Magnon man) was developed about 42,000 B.C. Thus, for only about 84 one-thousandth of one per cent of the whole span of creation is manifested any of its components which can with any directness point to a transcendent Reality in the universe. It is not surprising then that with recognition of such a vast extension of the pre-human part of the total time span, there has been a weakening of faith in God as heretofore conceived. The increasingly prevalent reaction to the scientific data is well summed up by Professor Carl Sagan of the Harvard University Department of Astronomy and a staff member of the Smithsonian Astrophysical Observatory:

> As science has progressed during the last few centuries, areas which were originally the exclusive province of religion have been increasingly preempted by science. We no longer hold that the Earth is stationary, or that it is at the center of the universe; nor that the world was made even approximately on October 23, 4004 B.C.; nor that it was made in seven days; nor that different species had separate creations; nor that the origin of the solar system and the origin of life are forever beyond the ken of man. Rather, the laboratory synthesis of life from materials which were abundant in the early environment of the Earth seems no more than a decade off. One result of these encroachments by science has been that there seems less and less for God to do. If he creates some hydrogen at the beginning of the universe, and establishes the physical laws, he

[43] Among scientists there is more modesty in this regard than has been displayed by theologians. For example, the Most Rev. James Ussher, the Anglican Archbishop of Armagh and Primate of All Ireland, dates the beginning of creation October 23, 4004 B.C., and dates with similar precision all principal events recorded in the Bible (*Annales Veteris et Novi Testamenti,* 1650–54). Until very recently his dating was accepted by the reference Bible which is authoritative for a considerable proportion of the Christian population in this country. However, in the current revision "Ussher's Tables" have been dropped in *The New Scofield Reference Bible* (New York: Oxford University Press, 1967), but not without alarmed protest from some "fundamental" Christians (see *Christian Century,* May 3, 1967, p. 582).

can then retire. He is a *roi faineant*. If God did not directly make life or man, it is hard to believe that he will intervene in our everyday lives, or answer our supplications.[44]

There is no question but that the advances of astronomical, geological, paleontological, and anthropological knowledge have contributed to the demise of the "God in the gaps" and to a serious undermining of the doctrine of Special Providence. But even with respect to a concept of God freed from the more obviously anthropomorphic cause-and-effect assertions, these advances should cause us to consider qualifying what have heretofore been regarded as eternal and unlimited attributes. There are those who affirm the existence of God—and with transcendent meaning—who explicitly limit the applicability of this hypothesis to the brief period since the emergence of man. Dr. W. F. Loomis makes the distinction precise by the use of the titles "God$_A$" and "God$_B$." He says:

Nature is there, and always will be, but nature is not man, and has no thoughts or desires, and is by no means in man's image. . . . [F]irst came Nature (or God$_A$), that set the stage for *Homo sapiens* to play his part. Nature made man, and man is part of Nature, but beyond this blind, unthinking force, came a new God$_B$ emerging from God$_A$. This is the God that lives in human hearts and molds their beings. From earliest times the two Gods have been confused. . . .

The story of [God$_B$] begins when Nature first evolved a talking, thinking creature on Earth that, by natural selection, competed with its less brainy neighbors for food and life, and so bred upwards until modern *Homo sapiens* appeared, about 40,000 years ago.[45]

Taking us back to merely a million years ago, at the beginning of the Pleistocene or Ice Age era, when "we would find a world

[44] I. S. Shklovskii and Carl Sagan, *Intelligent Life in the Universe* (San Francisco: Holden-Day, Inc., 1966), p. 19.

[45] *The God Within*, with foreword by the present author (New York: October House, 1967), p. 6. Another excellent treatment is Chap. 1 on the "Evolution of Man" in Hawkes and Wooley, *op. cit.*, n. 42, Chap. 7. See also S. G. F. Brandon, *Man and His Destiny in the Great Religions* (Manchester University Press, 1962), pp. 6–30 ("The Emergence of Man's Evaluation of Himself").

rather like the one we now see, with wild horses grazing on
grassy meadows, squirrels gathering nuts in the fall, and all the
everyday round of life in the forests and meadows going on
very nearly as it does today in the few remaining places where
man has not intruded," he asks. "Where was 'God' in these days,
when no animal used words of any kind and the ideas of 'purpose,' 'goodness,' and 'truth' remained to be invented by man
as concepts in the uncertain future?"[46]

We can leave this question open and make an affirmation
about the universe as it now is: there is transcendence here and
now. We are not living then in the vast reaches of time of Dr.
Loomis' God$_A$ (incidentally, if we were living then the designation
God$_B$ would be applicable). We are living now. Just as we legitimately infer the *more* from the observable components which
make up a particular person so we can legitimately infer the
More from observable components which make up the universal.
In making this affirmation we can attribute to God no less than
those elements of transcendence embraced within the meaning
of the word "personal." To be personal means, among other
things, an eagerness to relate to persons, a readiness to reveal
oneself. The etymology of our word "reveal" is illuminating here.
It comes from the Latin *revelare* which means "to unveil" or to
disclose. The Greek word customarily translated "truth" ($\dot{a}\lambda\dot{\eta}\theta\epsilon\iota a$,
aletheia) also means literally "uncovering" or "unveiling."[47]

46 *Op. cit.*, pp. 4–5. This question is precisely the opposite of the reported interrogation of Job by God: "Where were you when I laid the
foundation of the earth? Tell me, if you have understanding. Who determined its measurements—surely you know! Or who stretched the line upon
it? On what were its bases sunk, or who laid its cornerstone, when the
morning stars sang together, and all the sons of God [heavenly beings:
see Gen. 6:4] shouted for joy? Or who shut in the sea with doors, when
it burst forth from the womb; when I made clouds its garment, and thick
darkness its swaddling band, and prescribed bounds for it, and set bars
and doors, and said, 'Thus far shall you come, and no farther, and here
shall your proud waves be stayed'?" (Job 38:1–11)—and similar questions
regarding various of the animals (Job 38:39–39:30).

47 See Charles P. Price, "Revealed Religion in an Age of Science," *Zygon
—Journal of Religion and Science*, Vol. ii, No. 1 (March, 1967), pp. 23 ff.,
at p. 27.

This aspect of the affirmation of a personal God can be correlated with what is one of the predominant characteristics of the transcendence of man and one which Michael Novak uses as the key to theistic belief, "the drive to understand."[48] Man shares with the animals consciousness; but he has the gift of self-consciousness and the capacity to reflect on himself, and through the same characteristic the capacity to reflect on external data which are experienced. Professor Novak sees this drive "manifested in intelligent attention, into dynamism of inquiry and in the restless urge to explore new horizons." He continues:

A man does not appear to be curious as a cat is curious, for the satisfaction of immediate interests. A man sometimes wishes to understand exactly how things are in themselves and apart from his immediate biases; how they tick and what makes them tick. He is sometimes interested in understanding how things are related to his sense-perception, interests, viewpoints, needs, both concretely and in the future or in general. At other times he is interested in how things are related to one another, apart from their relation to him: not in whether it appears to him that the sun goes around the earth, but in the sun's motion relative to the motion of the earth without reference to his point of observation. Through his drive to understand, a man is capable of discounting some of his limitations and interests for the sake of explanatory understanding. The scientific spirit, for example, is striking evidence of the objectivity pursued by the drive to understand, at the expense of other human interests.[49]

Father Bernard Lonergan, s.j., summarizes this drive as "the pure, the detached, disinterested, unrestricted desire to know." "Without it," he says, "there would be no real meaning for such phrases as scientific disinterestedness, scientific detachment, scientific impartiality. Inasmuch as this intellectual drive is dominant . . . in that measure the scientifiic observer becomes an incarnation of inquiring intelligence. . ."[50] The product of

---

[48] *Belief and Unbelief: A Philosophy of Self-Knowledge* (New York: Macmillan, 1965), especially pp. 101–6.

[49] *Ibid.*, p. 101.

[50] *Insight: A Study of Human Understanding* (London: Longmans, Green & Co., 1958), p. 74.

this drive can be *truth*[51] but not in the sense of finality. Presupposed in the effort is that the subject matter with which the drive is concerned actually exists, and the results of the functioning of the drive over and over again verify the assumption: for example, technology is consequent upon science. Understanding is translated into doing; and very often indeed what is done "works." This relation of the subjective activity and the objective reality is thus summed up by Professor Novak:

> Who am I? At least this: I am a subject, aware and alert; I sometimes understand; and I sometimes am able to support with reasons my claim to understand, thus fulfilling the conditions on which such a claim is acceptable, both by myself and others, "objectively." I am an intelligent subject, then, capable of objectivity.[52]

The same drive which has made science even a possibility has, ever since the emergence of *Homo sapiens,* focused on larger over-all meanings and has been fulfilled for various men "in a creed, a philosophy or entelechy, which for them was the final truth," as the late Professor Erwin R. Goodenough phrased it. He summarized:

> This drive to understand can be on the level of the simplest myth, as that a primeval turtle created the world or that the world is governed by a group of gods like the Olympians; or it can rise to the most abstract metaphysical or theological abstraction, . . . [53]

The latter category he tellingly labeled "polysyllabic mythology." And this, as we have seen at some length,[54] can indeed be the case when affirmations are made either on the basis of one or another of holy authorities uncritically accepted or on a basis of an immodest degree of extrapolation from real data—in other words, "over-belief." But the fact that the undisciplined

51 "The great ones . . . will never forget the principle by which science has introduced a new epoch in human evolution, that personal conviction must always be subject to correction in terms of new data or knowledge." Erwin R. Goodenough, *Zygon, op. cit.,* p. 21.

52 *Op. cit.,* p. 100.

53 "A Historian of Religion Tries to Define Religion," *op. cit.,* p. 17.

54 See Chap. IV, pp. 49–50, and pp. 134–36, above.

functioning of the drive to understanding has led to error and to nonsense does not require us to limit our recognition of its capacity merely to the collating of data externally observable. Nor should it bar us from seeing this drive, both as it functions in this more limited way and as it leads to plausible inferences accepted on faith, as being in itself a clue to unseen transcendent Reality as the matching objectivity for its subjectivity. As Dr. Goodenough said:

> If we ourselves no longer believe that the God of Einstein's universe is counting the hairs of our heads, or stands ready to move mountains into the sea if we ask it with sufficiently commanding a faith, the simple fact remains that we can still pray, can break down the pettiness of our ordinary lives in the reality of what seems to us a transcendent good. Socrates was killed, among other reasons, for taking the gods of Athens too lightly, but he never lost the vivid experience of the little presence within him.[55]

The belief of Socrates[56] and its internal data-basis is one recorded example of the generic category of religious experience (or "peak experience") which, as we have seen, has recurred in individuals in various times and places, within the context of various religious traditions (and apart from any) accompanied by various visionary images and none, both described and explained in varying ways, and on which have been freighted various mythologies and ontologies—or none.[57] In our analyses of the reports of such phenomena we not only affirmed the reality of the internal happening but argued against the making of an a priori assumption that there is no reality to which the basic internal apprehension might correspond. We are now ready to go further and affirm that there is Reality concurrent with such experiences. This is not to assess or to validate every such experience claimed. But it is to affirm that such experiences can be connected with Fact or, to put it more clearly, that there is actually One to which such internal phenomena

---

[55] *Op. cit.*, p. 21.
[56] See more fully the author's *What Is This Treasure*, Chap. 2.
[57] See n. 39, above.

are a pointer and response. What has already been accepted as valid in the sensing of the *more* beyond the specific components which make up an individual person and as the *More* in the universe which corresponds to the "drive to understand" in man seen as an intellectual activity, is thus affirmed as involved in personal religious experience. Such an affirmation of belief in God, far from being barred or gradually eroded by the progress of science, is in fact consistent with the methodology of science and with its operative assumption about the interconnectedness of reality in the universe. *The God* (whether called God$_B$ or by any other name, or by none) *which is inferred as the Transcendent in the observable universe is the same God of whom individual persons can become aware in specific internal experiences.*

This is why early in the chapter in commenting on Dietrich Bonhoeffer's observations that the possible reduction of "God" (because of science) had relevance only with regard to man's concern about death and guilt, while the first of these concerns—death—and the answers for it were excluded from necessary connection with belief in God, the second—guilt—was reserved for later analysis. Consideration of it is appropriate at this point.

A variety of human factors (and even nonhuman ones, including chemical factors) have provided the context for religious experience. One type of experience which has been noticeably common has been a sense of personal inadequacy— a sense often accompanied by the conviction that this is one's own fault. This can be stated as the gap between the *ought* and the *is*. Whatever the derivative of the given *ought*, however sound it may be, and however correct may be the person's assessment of the *is* of his behavior, the gap which he perceives between these two is the measure of his sense of guilt. In short, for him, ought − is = guilt. Following this sensing can come a definable moment in which this gap is closed. This is different from the making of a "good resolution" about the future and from "good works" intended to bridge the gap from his direction.[58] Rather, it is sensed that the gap is closed from the "other direction." This is called, both in Biblical and classical theological language, "justification by grace through faith."[59] This phrase stands for both (a) an ontological doctrine received by many an orthodox believer apart from—or even without—any actual personal internal specific moment of sensing, and often interlocking with a particular doctrine of the Atonement (for example, the substitutionary interpretation of Jesus' death on the Cross), and (b) the actual experience of the closing of the gap, and of the resulting erasure of a sense of guilt, in particular individuals aware of, and believing in, the doctrine, and also on the part of many others innocent of it or living within the framework of very different religious traditions. A broader scope for describing these phenomena than the doctrinal label referred to is the expression, informed by the analysis of the late Dr. Paul Tillich: "I accept myself because I am accepted though unacceptable."

Commonly arising from such a conviction is a new dynamic for attitude and action. A customary and appropriate word to describe it is "thanksgiving." Arising, too, can be a new sense of confidence in one's capacity to fulfill the norm. This motivation and confidence combined can result in an externally observable change in the pattern of behavior.

It can readily be granted that the report of an internal happening of this category, even when accompanied by objective data as to the external events of behavior, both preceding and

[58] Quaintly as it is worded, here both relevant and basically sound is Article XIV of the Articles of Religion (and words to similar effect in other Confessions of Faith) on "Works of Supererogation" where there is said, on the premise that the *ought* is a 100 per cent claim (see the author's *Doing the Truth*, revised edition [New York: Macmillan, 1965], Chap. 4): "Voluntary Works besides, over and above, God's Commandments, which they call Works of Supererogation, cannot be taught without arrogancy and impiety: for by them men do declare, that they do not only render unto God as much as they are bound to do, but that they do more for his sake, than of bounden duty is required: whereas Christ saith plainly, When ye have done all that are commanded to you, say, We are unprofitable servants."

[59] *Doing the Truth* (n. 58), Chap. 7.

following the sense of acceptance, does not entail the conclusion that God has been involved or even exists. Open is the alternative hypothesis that what went on inside the person is entirely subjective—though it be granted that an objective situation "conditions" the psychological impression and what arose from the latter was manifested in objective action. But on bases by now discussed fully enough, one can affirm by faith that, in such experiences—fully recognizing the subjective element—connection may be made with objective, though unseen, reality—an active personal Reality already there and ready for the connection made within the individual human psyche.

This example has been analyzed both to complete our comment on Bonhoeffer's illuminating statement, and for its own sake. However, as is evident from other instances of religious experience already discussed,[60] this is only one category of personal data supportive of the faith-affirmation. (In fact it represents an experience much more common among persons in the Judeo-Christian tradition and fairly rare among others, since our religious heritage is guilt-producing—soundly and/or unsoundly, healthily and/or unhealthily—in a way other systems of belief have not been.) But in this illustration two factors have been noted which are often resultants of other types of peak experience: new confidence and a new attitude resulting in a change of behavior. It would not be asserted that such are necessary ingredients of a varied religious experience, but when they are shown to have occurred, not only is there provided additional support for a positive assessment regarding the reality of the claimed "moment," but also they provide the principal basis for a valuation of the experience as healthy and constructive. It is thus we can in a measure at least implement the injunction, "Beloved, do not believe every spirit, but test the spirits to see whether they are of God" (1 John 4:1). Here, as in other connections we see the soundness of "Thus you will know them by their fruits" (Matt. 7:20).

Complementary to the positive inference from such internal-

60 See pp. 130 ff., above.

external data and to the inference of a *Unus* in the universe, on a basis of the intuition and working assumption that the latter is such, is the impression commonly received from the fact that there is a considerable measure of order in the world. Grounded in such observed order is a certain degree of predictability. It is on this order and predictability that both science and technology in good part rest. On data and inferences of this type there has been based one of the traditional "proofs" for the existence of God, the Argument from Design. But there are several difficulties with this as a proof or even as basis for a faith-affirmation.

First of all, it assumes a doctrine of mechanical cause and effect which no longer has high respect in either science or philosophy. More than that, the old "watch, hence watchmaker" argument seemed much more conclusive in pre-Darwinian times when direct Divine creation of various items in the universe was assumed and when the process was cabined in a relatively short time-span, with the creation of man following in six days the beginning of the whole enterprise. As we have seen, there is very little in the process during the pre-human 99.9916 per cent of what appears to have been approximately the time-span to date, which reveals an underlying a priori pattern. Rather, what we see is a ponderously slow, inexplicable and hit-or-miss diversity of development, with many a false start.[61] Evidence of purpose and a consciously ordered process comes with man's emergence. Further, much (some would say all) of what we call "order" is actually the imposition upon data of humanly developed categories as bases for organized thought and experimental action. Finally, it is all too evident that— man in the universe or no—there is a vast amount of disorder, indeed chaos—much of it highly inconvenient to man's programming for happiness and security.[62]

Yet in his awareness of the amount of order there is, and of beauty, of joy and love, man here also frequently—in all cul-

[61] Cf. the outcome reflected in the quotation from Job in n. 46, above.
[62] See pp. 173–76, above.

tures and eras—experiences a distinct response, a yes-saying
accompanied by an intuitive attribution of immediately perceived phenomena to Someone or something imaged as
"beyond." Such repeated responses do not prove the existence of
God nor do they establish His nature or relationship to the
world; nevertheless they are connected with eternal Reality.
While this category, with its multitudinous instances, would
not—standing alone—provide a solid basis for a faith-affirmation, it nevertheless is in the realm of the empirical and
has a place alongside the other types of experiential response we
have surveyed as forming a wider base for a faith-affirmation
which relates *all* this to one ultimate Reality.

Nothing which has been said, nor any inferences made,
have foreclosed what has long appeared to be a basic question
about the *Unus* on which major world religions have divided.
The question is this: Is there a dichotomy between Creator and
creature, between God and each of the respective items in the
universe, *or* are each of the particular items continuous with
the One? With considerable consistency the "religions of the
book"—Judaism, Christianity, and Islam—have affirmed the
first hypothesis; with a similar degree of consistency the principal Oriental religions—Hinduism, Buddhism, and Taoism—
affirm the latter hypothesis.

The two positions can be described as dualism and non-
dualism. We will avoid the term "monism," because it can
imply pantheism, which—contrary to the assumption of many
in Western religions, including clergy—is not taught by the
Oriental religions. Pantheism means that there is no distinction
between the various beings, personal and nonpersonal, whereas
actually this distinction is recognized in all the religions mentioned, Eastern and Western. The non-dualism of the Eastern religions is more accurately denoted as *panentheism*. A homely
illustration of its import is seen in the distinctness from others
of each of the five fingers of a hand and the continuity of each
finger with the hand. Both for clarity and for more specific
relevance at this point, it could be put this way: each person

has a distinct autonomous existence, both physically and spiritually, as against every other human being; but each person is in continuity with the One—indeed *is* the One.

As we have seen there is a generic character to the mystical experience of, say, a Christian and a Zen Buddhist, and in the experiential patterns of persons of both traditions can be observed common factors. This is illustrated by the fact that present-day Zen Buddhist philosophers use the same Greek word as is used by both Paul and Western theologians to describe a process which experience—in East and in West—has been found to be a principal route to the consummation of personal fulfillment. The word is κένοσις, kenosis, that is, self-emptying.[63] The process and outcome bear different names in the two traditions: "salvation" in the Occident and "enlightenment" in the Orient, the difference being quite appropriate to the distinction between a dualistic and a panentheistic outlook on the ultimate Reality. A decision between these two alternatives and even concerning the basis on which one would proceed to decision as a basis for a faith-affirmation[64] is not easy. It is very difficult for a product of Western civilization to think other than in dualistic terms. We know that dualism is actually less extensive than we had heretofore thought: the matter-energy dichotomy is gone with the reduction of basic physical reality to energy; and the body-mind/soul dualism has, as we have seen,[65] been undermined by increased knowledge of psychosomatic connections. Yet even in these areas most people continue to think and talk in terms of the old pairs of concepts. Similarly, this would be somewhat true even if one had become fairly convinced of the panentheistic world-view. As a matter of fact, many Buddhists, especially those with Western ethnic background or who are

[63] See also pp. 110 and 130, above.
[64] For a compact analysis of the question with some of the implications of its being answered either way, see the author's *What Is This Treasure,* pp. 45–47, note; see the more complete treatment in Bishop John Robinson's 1966 Stanford Lectures, to be published in the fall of 1967 under the title *Exploration into God* by the Stanford University Press.
[65] See pp. 90–92, above.

resident in countries like the United States, commonly use the word "God," both in philosophical dialogue and as the name for the Focus of their devotion and religious experience. Therefore, it need not be too disturbing for one to recognize that in affirming belief in a personal God he may still be unable to reach a solid conviction as to whether God is "wholly Other" or is in some integral sense continuous with the universe.

The same consideration applies to another apparent dichotomy which is now coming more to the fore, though one which from an existential point of view—man's actual relationship to the divine Reality—is a very old dichotomy and one very significant in the earliest days of Christianity. The problem is this: Is God to be conceived of primarily as *being* or as *becoming*? In conventional Christian theology the former emerges totally prevailing, in whatever form it has been stated. Attributed to God as from everlasting and unto everlasting—has been omnipotence, omniscience, omnibenevolence. Entailed in such affirmations is a view of God as Being, with no logical room for the slightest degree of becoming. In contrast to this prevalent view has been the "process philosophy" of the late Alfred North Whitehead, Charles Hartshorne, Edgar S. Brightman, Shubert Ogden, and John B. Cobb, Jr.[66] Under this view, to whatever degree God is viewed as separate from or continuous with the evolving reality, He is conceived of as Himself in process and/or the Process itself. Again, as in the case of the dualism/nondualism conception, the being/becoming contrast is not easy to resolve. But the ultimate significance of the choice is less crucial for those who have moved from ontological to an existential mode of theological thought. Whatever might be ultimately the case, the fact is that the most significant avenue for man's intuitive and reflective perception of God is, especially in our era, the ever rapidly increasing display of transcendence on the part of man himself. So, focusing on man's data for affirmation about God and the stimulus to men's role as evolvers of reality,

[66] For a recent application see the latter's "Speaking about God," *Religion in Life*, Vol. xxxvi (Spring, 1967), pp. 28–39.

becoming is what can be most suitably affirmed. Thus Leslie Dewart, a Roman Catholic Professor at the University of Toronto, while foreclosed by his existentialist philosophical base from affirming Divine omnipotence, can confidently affirm the radical openness of history which not even man's misuse of freedom can block, and say:

... Once it no longer has "God's omnipotence" to fall back on, our Christian conscience may be awakened to feel its adult responsibilities for taking the full initiative in "restoring all things in Christ" and for exercising its creative ingenuity in order to determine how this should be done. For we will then no longer expect miracles to happen (least of all the miracle of the glorious appearance of the Christ upon a cloud), and we will instead believe that, unless we make it be, the Kingdom of God shall never come.[67]

Father Johannes B. Metz, a creative German Roman Catholic theologian, reminds us that Yahweh is more appropriately translated, not as "I am who I am" (Exod. 4:14, R.S.V.), but as "I will be what I will be," and that man must be making true the doctrines which he affirms. Thus an appropriate (though over-simplified) answer to the proclamation that God is dead is *He was never more alive.* And one whose approach is existentialist could react to the position of Dr. Loomis that God$_B$ emerges from God$_A$ only with the evolution of *Homo sapiens* with, "I pass," or "No comment." In any case it is *now* that we are living and can relate to God and share with Him in His ongoing creative process.

Finally, this last issue, and the possibility of a viable neutrality on it, throws light on the significant eschatalogical/gnostic controversy in very early Christianity.[68] The *gnosis*-minded emphasized that the saving Reality was already fully available, and developed variant and complex systems for the individual to partake of it. The *eschaton*-minded stressed that though we enter now into involvement with God through Christ, his fulfillment actually awaits that which is to come; and the details of

---

[67] *The Future of Belief* (London: Herder & Herder, 1966), pp. 193–94.
[68] See pp. 45–47, above.

the historically conceived future were variously and complexly spelled out. In terms of ontology these contrasting views (presumably after each has been considerably "pruned" by the now customary processes of demythologization) would definitely call for intellectual and personal decision. But under an existentialist approach this would not appear to be the case. For it can be a both/and rather than an either/or.

Suggestive is the important distinction on the part of current nonconformists in our society between the two types of -ins. Various forms of demonstrations have been engaged in, in the drive for a better future; for example, "sit-ins," "bank-ins," "teach-ins." But newer on the scene is the "be-in." Here there is focus on no particular cause (like civil rights, peace in Vietnam, or academic freedom). Rather, people just gather, more or less impromptu, in such locales as a park, beach, or house for a celebration of joy in one another's presence, conversation, and singing—all to the end of expressing and cultivating loving friendship. Both types of "-ins" are "demonstrations"; many of the same people are involved in each; no decision is called for as between these formats.

The same is true as to the basic approaches represented by *gnosis* and eschatology. Reflection upon, and inference from, the data of experience point to two things: We can even now become increasingly open, free of idolatrous blocks, and whole, open to the fulfillment by God acting within us (or, we could say, being "enlightened" as to the fact of our continuity with Him). At the same time we can focus toward the future—conjoining our energies, capacities, and insights (to whatever degree we have become whole and fulfilled) to the making of that which shall be. As Father Metz has put it, two thirds of faith is hope.

INDEX

Format by Sidney Feinberg
Set in Linotype Primer
Composed, printed and bound by The Haddon Craftsmen, Inc.
HARPER & ROW, PUBLISHERS, INCORPORATED